THE PRESENTING COACH

Tricia Woolfrey

First published in Great Britain in 2014 by Hodder & Stoughton. An Hachette UK company.

First published in US in 2014 by The McGraw-Hill Companies, Inc.

This edition published 2014

Copyright © Tricia Woolfrey 2014

The right of Tricia Woolfrey to be identified as the Author of the Work has been asserted by her in accordance with the Copyright, Designs and Patents Act 1988.

Database right Hodder & Stoughton (makers)

The *Teach Yourself* name is a registered trademark of Hachette UK.

British Library Cataloguing in Publication Data: a catalogue record for this title is available from the British Library.

Paperback ISBN 978 1 473 60128 4

Library of Congress Catalog Card Number: on file.

10 9 8 7 6 5 4 3 2 1

The publisher has used its best endeavours to ensure that any website addresses referred to in this book are correct and active at the time of going to press. However, the publisher and the author have no responsibility for the websites and can make no guarantee that a site will remain live or that the content will remain relevant, decent or appropriate.

The publisher has made every effort to mark as such all words which it believes to be trademarks. The publisher should also like to make it clear that the presence of a word in the book, whether marked or unmarked, in no way affects its legal status as a trademark.

Every reasonable effort has been made by the publisher to trace the copyright holders of material in this book. Any errors or omissions should be notified in writing to the publisher, who will endeavour to rectify the situation for any reprints and future editions.

Typeset by Cenveo® Publisher Services.

Printed and bound in Great Britain by CPI Group (UK) Ltd., Croydon, CRO 4YY.

Hodder & Stoughton policy is to use papers that are natural, renewable and recyclable products and made from wood grown in sustainable forests. The logging and manufacturing processes are expected to conform to the environmental regulations of the country of origin.

Hodder & Stoughton Ltd

338 Euston Road

London NW1 3BH

www.hodder.co.uk

CONTENTS

This book is dedicated to four groups of people:

To those people who were honest enough to give me feedback about my own presentation skills so that I could improve.

To the myriad of associates I have had the pleasure of working with who inspired me with their presentations, as well as some truly inspirational speakers at the innumerable courses and seminars I have attended over the years, and especially Ian McDermott (who taught me advanced level NLP through ITS), Robert Dilts and Marianne Williamson.

I also dedicate the book to my godsons, Thomas and Jeremy Crinall, who moved me to tears and laughter during their wedding and best-man speeches.

Finally, to my brother Will who did the most awesome eulogy for our father.

MEET THE COACH

Tricia Woolfrey is an integrative Executive Coach, Business Coach and Therapist with a background in Human Resources, Training and Coaching, Hypnotherapy and Nutrition.

As an expert in the psychology and physiology of behaviour, performance and productivity, she has a passion for helping people live a successful, fulfilled and balanced life. A proponent of mindfulness and heart-centred living, she works with corporate and private individuals wanting to get the most from their career and personal life.

She has a business consultancy and a hypnotherapy/nutritional practice in Harley Street, London, and in Surrey. She deals with groups and people on a one-to-one basis.

She runs numerous workshops for presentation skills, influencing skills, time management, personal development, stress management, anger management, performance, productivity and wellness.

She has three other books to her name as well as a number of CDs and MP3s. For more information, visit:

www.pw-consulting.co.uk

www.yourempoweredself.co.uk

www.self-help-resources.co.uk

www.triciawoolfrey.com

ACKNOWLEDGEMENTS

From all of you I have learned so much, and I shall remain eternally grateful.

Specific thanks go to the following people who gave me their insights, perspective and support on this exciting subject:

- Alan Donegan of Enjoy Presenting
- Constance Lamb of Constance Lamb Associates
- David Roylance of David Roylance Associates
- Ian Crocker of Absolute Learning
- Ian McDermott of International Teaching Seminars
- Neal Gandhi of Quickstart Global
- David North of Woby
- Robin Adams of PerfectBlend Video
- Simon Jordan from Simon Jordan Marketing

And finally to my husband, Tom, who provided a sounding board and support throughout.

It has been fun – thank you!

FOREWORD

I think you can make a strong case for saying that the most common fear in the world is the fear of public speaking. For many people the very phrase is enough to make them feel a little queasy. Whether it's the proverbial best man speech or a presentation at work that is coming up, many people quake at the prospect. And that's a shame because it really doesn't have to be that way.

When professionals talk about 'the art of presentation' the danger is it can sound as though there is some contrivance, even artificiality, about it. But being able to present well is really about being authentic and having something to say worth listening to. Far from requiring a person to learn slick tricks, it actually starts from inside you.

What do you really want to say? What really matters to you? What do you want the others to *get*? These are the questions I ask the people I work with when preparing them to step up and speak out. I need to know what's significant to the speaker. Above all, though, the would-be speaker needs to know! Often by telling me they clarify their own understanding of what they feel is most important to get across.

And this is true regardless of content or context. Those same three questions need to be answered whether you want to wow the Board or ask someone to marry you.

That's why I welcome the addition of this workbook to my bookshelf. Tricia Woolfrey has demystified much of the mechanics of presenting but never falls into the trap of making things mechanical. Throughout I have the sense that while she is explaining the how-to's that can make all the difference we never lose sight of the person, the presenter who's going to be making use of them. These helpful hints are presented in bite-sized chunks which I think is important because it makes learning manageable.

To do this Tricia has drawn on some of the best work in NLP to demystify the art of great presenting. NLP – Neuro Linguistic Programming – seeks to find models of excellence and unpack just what it is they do that makes them outstanding. Why? So that we can then make these skills available to a larger public. At its best this is a profoundly democratic demonstration of knowledge transfer. It is based on the principle that everyone can raise their game when they are given the how-to's.

So often people have aspirations but lack the how-to's that provide the means to achieve these dreams. When you look at a good recipe you're being given a step-by-step sequence that makes it possible for you to replicate the success of another. Recipes, of course, are not confined to cooking – people are sometimes asked about their recipe for success, for instance.

What you have here can truly be called recipes for success. However, while they make good servants they would make a bad master. Ultimately any recipe is only as good as the cook. And that is where you, dear reader, come in. These techniques are only going to deliver their full potential if they are in service of something bigger – and you must decide what.

So as you begin this workbook let me ask you to bear in mind a question. And it's this. If you were to master presenting, how would you be more able to be yourself? That's the real prize.

Ian McDermott

www.itsnlp.com

HOW TO USE THIS BOOK

This book will help you achieve presentation excellence and avoid some of the most common presentation howlers. It contains interactive exercises to help you develop self-insight and your presentation skills so that you feel more confident in how to put a presentation together and how to deliver it. There may be some chapters you can miss out, such as Chapter 5, if your focus is on business presentations. However, overall, it is best if you go with the flow of the book and complete all the exercises as you go along.

The book first of all describes the different kinds of presentations from business to social, their purpose and challenges. This gives you a general context for what follows which will be a more detailed look into what you will be required to do. There are chapters on business presentations, elevator pitches and social speeches.

In Chapter 6, you will discover the importance of knowing your audience.

Once you are clear about the context of your presentation and your audience, it is then important to think about the outcome, the structure and the content which will be covered in Chapter 7.

Chapter 8 is devoted to the use of visual aids. In Chapter 9 we will look at how to deal with presentation nerves. When you can do this effectively you are in a better position to engage and influence your audience which will be dealt with in Chapter 10.

Chapters 11 and 12 deal with the practicalities of your presentation and then, possibly the worst part in terms of what concerns people in presenting, dealing with the unexpected, including hiccups and hecklers.

There are lots of resources in the Appendices including checklists to help you make the best out of your presentations.

Do have a pen with you to complete the exercises. You might also want to have a highlighter pen to emphasize the points that have particular resonance for you. In this way you engage more with the content, you will absorb the information more easily and you can flip right back to the salient points whenever you need to.

In the meantime, remember that excellence is not an accident. To be a great presenter requires practice and persistence. Do engage fully with this book and be diligent in applying what you learn so that you can achieve excellence in your presentations.

1 INTRODUCTION

 OUTCOMES FROM THIS CHAPTER

- In this chapter we will identify the four worst types of presenter, and reveal the results of a survey on how people really feel about presenting, and what they expect from presentations. You will also have an opportunity to take the survey yourself and to do a self-assessment for some self-insight.

PRESENTATIONS ARE A WASTE OF TIME

Most people who have sat through presentations will have said this to themselves at one time or another. And they *are* a waste of time if they don't have the appropriate level of preparation and quality of delivery. However, with good planning and an eye for the audience, they can be one of the most effective ways of influencing, of informing and of entertaining.

This book is designed to help you overcome any fears or concerns you may have about doing a presentation – formal or informal, business or social.

In it you will learn tools and techniques to help you practically and emotionally so that you can present yourself and your subject at your best, in a way that you can enjoy. Because, when you enjoy your presentation, your will audience enjoy it too. You will come across as knowledgeable, authentic and credible.

This book will teach you how to get positive results confidently.

Whether you are an experienced presenter who wants to improve your skills, or a novice wanting to get it right first time, this book will help you to:

- prepare an effective presentation
- present to an audience with confidence and style
- use skills to ensure a positive result from your presentations
- enjoy your presentation
- deal with hecklers effectively.

When referring to an unnamed individual, we will use the terms 'him/his/he' as it will be easier to read than 'him/her', 'his/hers' and 'he/she'. We do hope that it will not interfere with your enjoyment of the book.

THE FOUR WORST TYPES OF PRESENTER

There are so many styles of poor presentation, but they fall into four main categories:

1 The Waffler

This presenter has no clear message, no structure and no clear outcome. He will tend to be monotone with poor eye contact. He will also tend to use 100 words (or, heaven forbid, 200 words) where ten will do, thereby leaving the audience dazed and confused.

2 The Preener

This presenter loves the limelight and uses the opportunity of having an audience as a means to indulge this desire for attention. His preening will mask his message and his over-inflated view of himself will fool him into thinking the audience will want more, so he will happily overrun.

3 The Slideshow Bore

This presenter will have an abundance of slides, with too much information and too many special-effects, both sound and visual. He will be more interested in looking at his beautiful slideshow than in connecting with the audience who will become intimately acquainted with his back rather than his message.

4 The Deer in the Headlights

This person starts his presentation in fear and ends in relief. He will engender a mixture of pity and scorn from the audience. He will frantically search the audience for a friendly face and fixate upon it, thereby alienating everyone else – a fact of which he will be blissfully unaware.

COACH'S TIP

Prepare well

Unless you are clear of your outcome, prepare appropriately and deliver the presentation in an engaging way, you will lose your audience and, potentially, your reputation.

Presentations can be fun! What gets in the way is presenting with a negative mindset. If you find yourself dreading presentations, this is likely to spill out into your communication and can inhibit your message.

WHAT YOU WILL LEARN

Presentations – offline and online, to small audiences and large – are more and more important in terms of communication, impact and influencing. So, in this book, you will learn:

- Preparation:
    - Mind – getting your head in the right space so you feel confident and in your 'flow'.
    - Subject – so you know what you're talking about.
    - Structure – so there is a logical sequence to take the audience to where you want them to be.
    - Practical – the nuts and bolts of getting your presentation off to a good start and a good ending.
- How to use visual aids and other tools for the job.
- How to create impact so that people take you seriously without you having to get too serious.
- How to understand your audience – when you know their agenda and their hot buttons your ability to influence your outcome increases exponentially.
- How to deal with difficult people so that hecklers can be a boon rather than a bane.
- How to think on your feet so that no matter what curve balls come your way, you can deal with them with grace and ease.

COACHING SESSION 1

Presentations and you

First of all, why not take this quiz so that you can better understand your feelings about presenting. Tick the box that most represents your feelings:

1. To what degree are presentation skills important in your work?

   a Very important ☐

   b Important ☐

   c Helpful ☐

   d Not important at all ☐

2. To what degree are presentation skills important as part of your future career plans?

   a Very important ☐

   b Important ☐

   c Helpful ☐

   d Not important at all ☐

3. How would you currently rate your presentation skills?

   a Excellent ☐

   b Accomplished ☐

   c Passable ☐

   d Plenty of room for improvement ☐

   e Don't know ☐

4. How do you feel about the prospect of doing a presentation?

   a Brilliant – can't wait ☐

   b OK – not a problem ☐

   c Oh no – do I have to? ☐

   d ?!* – how am I going to get out of this? ☐

5. Have you ever made excuses to get out of doing a presentation?

   a Yes ☐

   b No ☐

If yes, why?

What impact did it have on your work?

6. What impact did it have on your relationships at work?

7. What impact did it have on your self-esteem?

8. What concerns you most about presenting?

   a Nothing ☐

   b Forgetting what I want to say ☐

   c Getting my message across clearly ☐

   d Knowing how to structure the presentation well ☐

   e Using technology ☐

   f Overrunning ☐

   g Being judged ☐

   h Being taken seriously ☐

   i Blushing ☐

   j Shaking ☐

   k Other ☐

9. What was the worst presentation you have ever witnessed? What made it so bad?

10. What was the best presentation you have ever witnessed? What made it so good?

11. What does all of this say about what you want to learn from this book?

PRESENTATIONS – A JOURNEY

The author would like to share with you her journey as a presenter as an example of how it is possible, even in the most improbable of situations, to become a proficient and skilful presenter:

As a child I was always shy and self-conscious. I used to dread being asked to read aloud in class and I would stumble on my words and speak without inflection – my voice a monotone series of unconnected words. I would marvel at the blonde-haired swot whose name was Diana. She was absolutely brilliant at reading out loud and would make whatever she was reading sound interesting. She seemed entirely unperturbed by the sea of faces pointing in her direction and seemed calm and engrossed in the activity, just as her audience were calm and engrossed.

Oh, how I wished I was more like her.

However, this contrasts with a smaller part of me who, years earlier, would sit on the playground floor telling stories to a small but growing audience. These were fairy tales that I would adapt with surprising twists and turns, making the audience laugh and ask for more.

It got to the point where people would approach me and ask for a story and somehow I would conjure one up out of nowhere. It was an enjoyable part of my school life which preceded the 'reading-out-loud phase'.

The 'reading-out-loud phase' was in senior school where I now realize I became more self-conscious as people became more competitive and judging and so I retreated into myself, judging myself before others did.

Then came the world of work. For the first few years I was not required to present anything apart from my name and where I was from when I attended a course. Like most people, I found this to be embarrassing and my tummy would perform all kinds of gymnastics until my turn was over. You'd think I had been asked to address the G8 summit with a peaceful solution to terrorism in three easy steps.

Those stomach-churning moments became a feeling to avoid and the only way of doing that was to avoid the limelight, which I was more than happy to do.

However, as my career progressed, I was required to present as part of my job. As a person with an over-developed sense of duty and responsibility, I would perform this function with dread, feeling worse each time as I came to realize, with the clarity of a freshly cleaned pair of spectacles, that a good presenter I was not.

It came to a head one day when, having spent some time in the toilet being ill, I got on stage and delivered the required presentation dutifully.

I was approached afterwards by kind-hearted souls who said 'never mind' or similar words of reassurance and comfort. Clearly, my nerves and ineptitude were visible to all and sundry.

I pondered this sad state of affairs. What was wrong with me? I was intelligent, I knew my stuff, and I even knew practically everyone in the audience, having hired most of them myself. Why did I get into such a state?

I realized that I had thoughts running through my mind so debilitating and so fast, that there was no chance any sensible communication could be transmitted to or be received by my bemused audience. What was I saying to myself?

'Oh no, everyone's looking at me.'

'Will I remember everything?'

'What will they make of what I have to say?'

'I wish I was as good as x, y, and z – they're brilliant presenters.'

'I'm the worst presenter here today.'

'I'm boring.'

'HR is boring.'

'Why can't I smile properly when people are looking at me expectantly?'

'My voice is shaking.'

'I sound like an idiot.'

'I look like an idiot.'

'How much time do I have left?'

'I wish I was a street-sweeper, then I wouldn't have to do any of this stuff.'

'What's *wrong* with me?'

It is no wonder that my presentations were poor, my message unclear and my audience bored, if not kind.

But how could I extricate myself from this without extricating myself from the career I enjoyed in every other respect?

I reflected on what was happening, on the difference between me in my 'story-telling phase' and my 'reading-out-loud phase' and realized the difference was in my focus. I had moved from outward focus to inward focus and the effect was crippling. Here are my observations:

1. I was focusing far too much on people looking at me and judging me.

2. I enjoy helping people.

3. I like the people in the audience.

4. I know my stuff.

So, from that point onwards, I decided to empty my mind of all the negative thoughts that clouded my thinking (it's easier than you think).

While I would prepare fully, I gave myself permission to make mistakes and to use humour if that happened (a great skill I developed in my 'story-telling phase').

Then I would connect with the audience by looking at the individuals I knew and liked so well and simply shared information that I knew would help them.

That was it. My attention moved from self-oriented to other-oriented, I engaged my humour and the transition from 'the deer in the headlights' to 'accomplished presenter' was made.

Am I the best presenter you've ever seen? No. But I'm good and that's good enough for me. I do get lots of compliments about how confident and engaging I am when presenting – a huge change from the 'never-mind' that I used to get!

 COACH'S TIP

What makes a good presenter?

When you think about what makes a good presenter, it will be someone who is confident in themselves, their subject, their body language and voice, who is articulate, has good rapport with their audience and who is a clear communicator, making their message interesting and compelling. A good presenter will also be organized, structured and keep to time.

COACHING SESSION 2

Presentation self-assessment

Complete this quick self-assessment to see where you are:

	Terrible	Need improvement	Not bad	Quite good	Excellent
Suitably dressed and well groomed					
Confident					
Appear relaxed and natural					
Good rapport with the audience					
Excellent eye contact					
Positive body language					
Appropriately facially expressive					
Lack of distracting habits					
Voice: Pace, Pitch, Projection, Pauses and Precision					
Articulate					
Make points clearly					
Free from uhs, ers, ahs, you-knows and likes					
Handle questions well					
Well prepared					
Well organized					
Good structure					
Message is interesting and compelling					
Good and appropriate use of humour					
Keep to time					
Involve audience appropriately					
Deal with difficult people appropriately					
Good use of visual aids					

Given your self-assessment, what do you want to focus on as you read this book?

(See Appendix 12 for checklist.)

ONLINE RESOURCE

Presentation self-assessment

A downloadable version of this template is available for your use from

www.TYCoachbooks.com/Presenting

SURVEY RESULTS

A survey revealed that 43 per cent of presenters were not happy with their level of skill but 93 per cent felt that it was essential to their career. One in five people dread doing a presentation, with 14.5 per cent making excuses to get out of it.

By far the biggest concerns were:

1. Getting their message across clearly.

2. Remembering what to say.

3. Knowing how to structure the presentation well.

The survey also revealed that people enjoy audience participation, and a presenter who had a heart-connection with their message. They enjoy an element of surprise, humour and emotionally evocative messages.

They appreciate anecdotes and structure and slideware being a springboard for the presentation rather than the actual presentation itself.

The worst presentations were characterized by a lack of preparation, rushing through the end because they waffled at the beginning, and slides being read out verbatim. One person reported 'The presentation was on a subject that I knew little about and, by the end of the jargon-filled ramble, I still didn't have a clue.'

> *There are certain things in which mediocrity is not to be endured, such as poetry, music, painting and public speaking.*
>
> Jean de la Bruyère

 **NEXT STEPS**

In this chapter you have looked at what to expect from the book in terms of helping you to prepare an effective presentation and present with both confidence and style for a positive result for you and the audience. You have also learned about the four worst types of presenter: The Waffler; The Preener; The Slideshow Bore and The Deer in the Headlights. The quiz will have helped you to better understand your feelings about presenting so that you have more insight into yourself and the self-assessment featured will help you to clarify areas where you excel and where you need to improve. This will help you to focus your attention on the areas for improvement throughout the book. You have also looked at the survey results to see what people look for when they attend a presentation. Finally, you have had an overview of how the book is structured and how to use it to best effect.

In the next chapter you will look at the different types of presentation and their implications for you in terms of planning.

👍 TAKEAWAYS

This is your opportunity to take stock of what you have learned from this chapter. You might want now to choose other chapters and exercises to focus on, or you can continue to work through the whole book if this fits your needs more.

Which style of presenter did you most identify with?

What has been your own presentation journey?

What are the top three areas you need to focus on (from the self-assessment) that will have the biggest impact on your ability to undertake effective presentations?

1.

2.

3.

2 | TYPES OF PRESENTATION

✔ OUTCOMES FROM THIS CHAPTER:

- In this chapter we will learn about the different types of presentation including business updates, educational and inspirational. We will identify the purpose of each and understand the challenges they pose.

You may have purchased this book with a particular type of presentation in mind. Perhaps you have been called on to do a business update at a management meeting, or you want to become an inspirational speaker, or perhaps you want to get into marketing your business on YouTube.

! COACH'S TIP

Presentation principles

It doesn't matter how formal or informal your presentations will be, or whether you have 60 seconds or 60 minutes; impromptu or planned, there will be certain principles that apply to all presentations: rapport, clarity, thinking about your outcome, and use of voice and posture.

Increasingly, presentations are moving from the 'in-person' style, where you are physically in front of your audience, to remote presentations on webinars and videos. Whatever the context for your presentation, some common principles will always apply.

BUSINESS UPDATE

Business updates tend to be short but regular. A team of individuals, either across the whole company or organized around a particular project, get together to update each other on progress. These meetings can go on for a long time so people can get bored and are often thinking about what they are going to say when it's their turn instead of listening to what you are saying. The challenge, therefore, is to say what you need to say in a punchy, informative and engaging way. What is often neglected at these updates, which is often the underlying reason for them, is the interdependencies between one group and another and how what one person is doing can have a consequence for others.

PROPOSING CHANGE

Sometimes you will have to convince a group of people of a proposal for change, such as a new system, a restructure or relocation. This can be a very difficult presentation as many people resist change – they like to hold on to the familiar because it is comfortable. Change is one of life's few constants. Without it we would not have light, medicine or global travel. Change is an integral part of life. It is an essential part of business. However, it is often difficult to convince people of the need to make changes because it creates fear and requires effort. So a presentation about a proposed change should embrace what will remain the same, the consequences of delay or resistance, and the benefits of the change.

SALES

In a sales presentation, you may be presenting for the first time to people you have just met, or this may be the final stage in a long process. This will depend on the type of product you are selling and the type of business you are selling to.

If you are selling a widget to a local hardware store, you are likely to have one shot and it may be on the shop floor, so you need to be 'ready for anything'. If you are lucky, you will have a meeting room and be able to present in a more conducive environment. It may also be over the counter, with your 'audience' being interrupted by customers wanting to purchase something else, so you have to wait patiently for the transaction to finish before you can continue where you left off.

The challenge for this kind of presentation is to get your point across quickly, having the flexibility to stop and start with good grace and picking up where you left off, keeping your audience on track and maintaining rapport throughout.

However, if you are selling a complex technology solution to an organization, with a value of, say, £50,000, the presentation will be quite different. Because this will be seen as a significant investment to the business you are likely to have a number of people present, some of whom you will have never met such as the Finance Director and the CEO.

The aim here is to engage the different agendas for all the people present so they all see the benefits of your proposal. Juggling these different agendas elegantly is an art-form and it's important to keep eye contact with everyone otherwise rapport will be lost.

ELEVATOR PITCH

This is a subset of the sales pitch, where you have around 60 seconds to tell people about you and your business with the purpose of generating interest in your service or product. Although designed for networking meetings, they can be just as usefully employed when you are literally in an elevator – where you have a short amount of time to make an impact – or on a train as a conversation is struck up between yourself and a fellow passenger, or perhaps at a party to introduce yourself. You never know when you might meet a prospective client and so having an elevator pitch prepared will help you to best position yourself and your business to create potential sales in the most obscure of circumstances. The challenge is to be interesting without being pushy and creating a pitch that encourages people to find out more.

INVESTORS

This is the über-sales pitch. You aren't just getting people to buy into your product, but into you and your entire concept so that you can build your business. They are investing a great deal of money and, if they don't believe that you can deliver on your promise, you won't get the investment you are looking for. They need to know that you are passionate, intelligent, understand your market, have a clear strategy and have thought through the investment requirements – how you will use it, what return they will get and how quickly. More than anything, you need to be believable. Confidence, clarity and rapport are the key concepts to consider. Remember that their real interest is in what return they will get and whether they believe that you are the person to deliver that to them.

EDUCATIONAL

Educational presentations – training – teach a concept, a behaviour, a skill or a process and the audience can vary:

- **In-company** This is where the education may be on a product, process, skill, health and safety, or about the business.

- **Public courses** These might be for career development (such as a professional qualification, business skill or technical skill) or personal development (such as the myriad of NLP courses, confidence building, get-your-life-on-track courses that are available).

- **School, college, university** These are undertaken in a classroom environment to a specific curriculum, but still require good presentation skills.

In each case, it is important to consider two things:

1. The learning outcomes: what is it you want them to learn from the training. What is it you want them to walk away being able to do as a result of the training?

2. What is their learning style? Neuro Linguistic Programming – the science of achievement – informs us that there are four representational systems and that these link into how we take in information and learn:

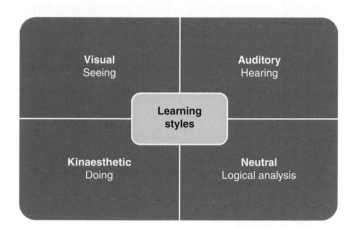

1. **Visual** – by seeing. This is why diagrams and graphs can be so useful. Having slides that support your message and are aesthetically pleasing is important. A busy slide will offend the eye of the visual learner.

2. **Auditory** – by hearing. For the auditory audience your voice is going to be your prime tool for ensuring your message gets across so a good voice with excellent intonation will be important.

3. **Kinaesthetic** – by doing: touch, practice, role playing, etc. Without this the kinaesthetic audience will find it hard to concentrate. They will ask lots of questions which is their way of connecting with the material.

4. **Neutral** – by the process of logical assessment and reflection. The neutral audience will need proof and time to reflect on what has been said. They love data.

Each of us has a preferred representational system, visual being the most common one. It's important to understand that people take in information in different ways and that, by focusing too much on one way, you are potentially diluting your message and 'losing' part of your audience. It is very easy to slip into your own representational system, so do be careful. The challenge is made more complicated if you are talking to a large group of people as there is likely to be a mixture of representational systems present.

Because this is such an important area, we will go into it more in Chapter 10.

INSPIRATIONAL

Inspirational presentations, or motivational talks, are becoming more and more popular and there is a plethora of them available on YouTube.

As the title suggests, the purpose is to motivate and inspire. An inspirational speaker is often hired at a corporate event as a headliner to motivate the employees, leaving them feeling energized and enthused. Inspirational speakers typically have a story to tell of triumph over adversity, they will be excellent rapport builders, and will generally have a lot of energy and enthusiasm which will be infectious. They will rarely use PowerPoint and, if they do, they will not be reliant on them to get their message across. They will be super-confident and will create a lively energy in the audience. They will tend to be either entertaining or thought-provoking, captivating the audience with their story or spurring them on to a new way of thinking, doing and being. This is not for the faint-hearted or the inexperienced.

An inspirational talk may also be required to encourage commitment to a course of action, as a politician would before an election, or a CEO may do when announcing an organizational change, or a manager may be required to do for his team.

INTRODUCING A SPEAKER

Sometimes a presentation is simply to introduce another presenter. However, it's still a presentation of sorts and requires a level of thought and skill. 'I would like to introduce you to ...' is OK, but it is a bit flat and makes it hard work for the next speaker to pick up that energy. It also wouldn't reflect too well on you. It's important to set the scene so that the speaker you are introducing has a strong foundation to build on.

SOCIAL

Social presentations can be anything from a eulogy, to a wedding speech, to a thank you. You can be really creative and have fun, or you can be very formal.

- **Eulogies** A lovely funeral the author went to had two eulogies: one created an unexpected but enjoyable burst of laughter at a story involving the deceased. It was warm-hearted and loving and yet very humorous. The second eulogy was very tender, involved a poem, and had the opposite effect – tears from the audience. Both were perfect yet the impact on the audience was quite different.

  Eulogies can be difficult to do as you might be feeling quite emotional on top of the regular nerves that most people will experience giving a presentation. The important thing to consider is how you want to honour the deceased in a way they would appreciate (depending on your beliefs, they may very well be watching!). Either way, you want to feel good about the way you represented them in this final goodbye.

- **Weddings** Wedding speeches, again, can induce laughter or tears. But, if you are thoughtful and plan well, they will not be tears of boredom. Humour, however, needs to be carefully judged since the audience will be mixed – the bride and groom generally will be young, but elderly relatives are likely to be present, as are children. So any humour should be suitable for a family audience and not cause offence.

- **Thank yous** Thank you speeches are sometimes impromptu – an unexpected award in front of an audience will give rise to an expectation of a speech from you. While they may be given in a business context, they are more social in nature. If you are lucky, you will know in advance that there will be a thank you to be given – perhaps if you are thanking people for their support for a charity event, or you are leaving a company and it is traditional to receive a parting gift. Or perhaps you are saying thank you to someone for their support on a specific project and you want to honour their contribution publicly.

Thank yous are lovely presentations to give. The challenge is to keep it short and light and sincere.

 COACH'S TIP

Social presentations

Social presentations can be light and humorous, or reflective and solemn.

WEBINARS

As a medium for promoting your business or conducting seminars over the internet, webinars are fast becoming the communication channel of choice for coaches and trainers. There are various challenges involved, however, from having the right technology, to achieving and maintaining rapport without having eye contact and maintaining interest with little evidence as to how your audience is reacting.

VIDEO

Optimizing your website is becoming more and more complex as we all compete for the same audience and video is widely considered as the best way of doing this at the time of writing. In addition, YouTube is a great way of delivering your message and of promoting your brand. The challenge is to make the video informative, entertaining and natural. Most people are nervous and stilted in videos. To be credible, it is important to adopt a relaxed and natural manner, making your audience feel as though you are directing your message to them personally.

RADIO

If you are to be interviewed on radio, you will normally have limited time to make your points and there is practically no scope for building rapport with the audience, though you will obviously want the interviewer on your side. Your challenge is to be super-focused on your outcome and make sure that you are speaking directly into the microphone. One movement of the head can spoil the effect altogether.

> *The greatest problem with communication is the illusion that it has been accomplished.*
>
> George Bernard Shaw

NEXT STEPS

In this chapter you have explored the different types of presentation, both formal and informal. These range from your elevator pitch to proposing an important change to a business, inspirational presentations to social ones, such as wedding and thank you speeches. You have also had a look at webinars, video and radio which are becoming ever-more important.

You have explored the different type of learning styles people have which, while important if you are giving any training, are equally important when considering your audience in other types of presentation.

You have learned that, no matter what the presentation, there are some principles that apply to all of them including rapport, clarity, outcome, use of voice and posture

In the next chapter you will learn in more depth about how to undertake effective business presentations.

TAKEAWAYS

This is your opportunity to take stock of what you have learned from this chapter. You might want now to choose other chapters and exercises to focus on, or you can continue to work through the whole book if this fits your needs more.

What kind of presentation do you/are you likely to get involved in?

What are the implications of this for you?

What worries you most about it?

What steps do you need to take to overcome these?

3 BUSINESS PRESENTATIONS

✓ OUTCOMES FROM THIS CHAPTER

- In this chapter we will look at the types, purposes and approaches to specific kinds of business presentation, including in-house, webinar, video, Skype and radio presentations, and those to investors, clients and prospects.

Having to do a business presentation is usually the reason people want to improve their presentation skills. Your ability to present effectively can inhibit or enhance your career. Presentations are a very visible indication of your knowledge, skills, potential and status. It is not surprising that people get nervous about them.

IN-HOUSE

There are two main types of in-house meeting.

All-employee meeting

This might be the annual kick-off where each department talks about their plans for the year ahead and the intent is to inform, inspire and educate. There is often a team-building element involved. And, of course, the party in the evening!

Typically there will be a round of departmental presentations and break-out meetings. Because there will be so many presentations, it is important that your message is not lost to a jaded audience. It is vital that you maintain the energy of the audience and the focus on your outcome.

An all-employee meeting might also be to announce a new product launch, a restructure, a merger or an acquisition.

Inter-departmental or departmental

This might be a regular meeting with a general update, or a meeting around a specific project. You will need to know the inter-dependencies of what you are talking about to everyone else. You also need to be attentive to what other people are saying as it may impact your presentation. Let's take an example:

Advanced Systems Corporation is introducing a new product line

Research and development are responsible for the design; manufacturing are responsible for production; sales are responsible for selling it to their existing clients and also to new prospects; presales are involved with adapting the solution and training the customers to use the product; customer services are involved with providing support; HR are involved in making sure there are sufficient trained and appropriately skilled people to fulfil each part of the project and the commission structure for it; marketing are involved in creating the demand and finance are responsible for the budgeting, invoicing and collections.

If one piece of that puzzle is out of synch, it affects everyone else, for example:

- If HR haven't hired the sales people needed to sell.
- If finance haven't apportioned or sanctioned sufficient funds.
- If research and development have a design fault.
- If manufacturing have a technical issue with production, etc.

Each element impacts everyone else. So, not only are these meetings a way of keeping people updated, they help to iron out any problems before they become crises.

COACH'S TIP

The bigger picture

In your presentation it is important to think about not just where you are, but how this impacts everyone else, what you might need from them, what they might need from you, and so on. So, as well as thinking about what you have to say, keep the bigger picture in mind so that your contribution has a more positive impact. This means that your listening skills during other people's presentations need to be fully engaged so that you are linking in as appropriate when your turn comes.

In-house meetings may cover, among other possibilities:

- performance against budget
- project update
- gaining commitment to a new initiative
- announcing a promotion, a new hire or a restructure

- announcing redundancies
- launching a new product
- training
- winning their hearts and minds for a more successful period ahead.

In addition, your choice of meeting room may reflect:

- availability of an in-house option suitable to the size and nature of your presentation
- the need for confidentiality.

In Chapter 10 we will look at how to put forward a business case.

CLIENTS AND PROSPECTS

This is tricky as you will often not know what kind of room you will be presenting in, nor whether the promised equipment will be a) available, b) working, and c) in a configuration that facilitates a smooth presentation. You often find that the projector is too close or too far away, or there is no room for your laptop or papers. In addition, you may be informed of who will be invited to your presentation but the actual audience may differ:

- Someone more senior may suddenly decide to attend.
- Someone important may be missing – they may be a big supporter or a decision maker.
- You may get an unexpected heckler or naysayer. If it is a sales presentation, this may be the Finance Director whose objective will be different to the buyers.
- You may get a large audience where you were expecting just two or three people.

If you have a lot of experience presenting in different places, you may be unfazed by the unpredictability of the circumstances surrounding the client presentation. However, if not, it is useful to:

- practise your presentation in different situations so that you have flexibility in your approach
- bring extra packs with you in case additional people arrive
- bring back-up materials such as a soft copy of your presentation saved to a memory stick, a hard copy with notes for you, a hard copy without notes for your audience in case they need to make copies
- bring your own laptop and power cable.
- consider your message for different audience members, for example:

- the Managing Director
- the Finance Director
- the Procurement Manager
- the HR Director
- the Line Manager
- the end-user
- the IT Manager

- think of all their differing agendas and how you might position your talk to include them. Let's take an example. Let's say you are selling a laptop:

  - The Managing Director will be concerned about what return on investment he will get for the business.

  - The Finance Director will be concerned about whether there is sufficient budget and if he can reduce the costs.

  - The Procurement Manager will be similarly concerned about budget and costs but also about contract terms, about your credentials as a supplier and whether you are on the preferred supplier list.

  - The HR Director will want to be aware of whether there will be any training or resourcing issues.

  - The Line Manager wants to know whether it is fit for purpose.

  - The end-user will be concerned with ease of use.

  - The IT Manager will want to know if it has the latest features and functionality.

 COACH'S TIP

Dealing with the unexpected

In your preparation, you will need to consider all the issues discussed here, in case you need to address them in the meeting. This will ensure that you are confident in the face of unexpected questions and other people's political agendas.

The difference between presenting to an existing client and a prospect is one of familiarity. An existing client will know both your product and you (unless you have replaced their previous contact). In any event, they are a better known quantity. However, there may be times when you are delivering contentious news (such as 'We can't fulfil your order as we promised'), or good news ('We have a new product version that we developed as a result of your feedback').

With a prospect, you are competing for their order. You may or may not have knowledge of what the competition has to offer so it is difficult to know how to pitch yours so you have a better chance of winning. It is easy to get bogged down with price being the most important differentiator but it's important to know that people buy from people. The most important thing you can do is come across as authentic, with a genuine interest in serving them. If they sense that your priority is to get them to sign the order before you leave because you have a quota to reach, you will be less likely to win it. If they sense that your primary purpose is that, following their procurement process, they have the solution they are looking for, whether it is with you or not, that can win you many points because it develops trust.

As previously discussed, in comparison to the existing client, you will not know the personalities involved, their individual agendas or the internal politics. Research is key and your ability to flex your style according to the situation will stand you in very good stead.

We will explore more about your message in Chapter 7, and in Chapter 10 we will look at how to talk in terms of features instead of benefits.

INTRODUCING A SPEAKER

If you are called on to introduce another speaker, this is still an opportunity for you to shine as an individual and so requires a little planning. This also helps the speaker begin from a point of strength.

Start with introducing yourself if you are there for the sole purpose of the introduction and the audience don't know you. Say a little about the reason for the event if it hasn't been explained already. A bit of background about your speaker and what they will be speaking about comes next. This should be an enthusiastic build-up so they come onto the stage to a warm and receptive audience.

If there are any slides, it is likely to be just the one with the person's name on it as they will probably also give some background themselves. It works really well where there is a link and the person thanks you and, during their talk, links in to some of the things you mentioned during your introduction. It is not intended as a scene-stealer but a scene-setter.

WEBINARS

Webinars are increasingly used as an efficient way of reaching a large group of people at low cost. They are also a useful marketing tool. However, there are some important principles to consider if you want to be successful as creating rapport and maintaining interest are challenging using this format.

You will need to have the right technology to deliver your webinar. Technology is changing all the time and there are numerous options available. Two of the most popular ones at the time of writing can be found at the following websites:

- www.gotomeeting.co.uk
- www.anymeeting.com

When looking for a provider, things to consider are:

- Do they enable you to upload your own presentation?
- Can you project your own video image?
- Does it allow you to conduct polls?
- Can you mute the audience?
- Does it allow you to share screens? (Useful if you want to demonstrate something on your own computer.)
- How does it handle questions from the audience?
- Does it enable you to record the webinar so you can send/sell the recording after the event?
- Can it handle the invitations and social media to promote the event?
- How much is it?
- Their support opening hours – beware of what time zone these refer to.

Your internet connection needs to be reliable – as does that of your audience. You may have the best presentation in the world but if your connection is weak or fails you, it is all for nought. It can be very frustrating for your audience who may experience time delays or poor screen/sound quality. Your webinar partner will be able to advise you on the specifications for your computer, web browser and connection to help you get the best results. It always helps to have all other applications closed so that you have maximum power and to avoid any possible software conflict. If your internet connection is wireless, it is likely to affect the speed of connection so do make sure you have a wired connection.

Creating rapport can be very difficult as the audience is faceless. For most people, eye contact, nods of agreement and smiles of approval from the audience all help to build confidence. None of this is possible on a webinar – in either direction, so it's important to make up for this in different ways. The first is chatting to the audience before the webinar begins as you might before a more conventional presentation. You will see names appear as your attendees sign-on, so you can welcome them personally. A way of losing rapport is to have a webinar title and then either make it an overt sales-pitch or overrun wildly. So do make sure that you explain at the beginning the purpose, structure and timing of the webinar so that they know what to expect. Do keep them updated about where they are in the process too.

If you don't engage your audience and provide value and interest throughout your webinar, they can easily sign off without fear of embarrassment. This happens if you are too salesy and self-promoting. It also happens if you overrun. It is essential that you are constantly providing value – the 'What's in it for me?' factor. Another way of maintaining interest is to use polls, encourage questions and even ask the audience to do a reflective exercise. For example, 'Write down the three main ideas you want to implement following this webinar.' Ask rhetorical questions – why? Because they maintain focus, they invite discussion. They are not intended to elicit a strict answer but to encourage communication and engagement. Do refer to your slides regularly to keep the audience focused on the screen. For example 'As you can see from this slide ...'. Finally, you may need to project your personality more than usual because you do not have the luxury of body language to make your point.

Keep it natural – reading out a script will sound like you are reading out a script and you will lose your audience very quickly. Practising is really key here. Make sure you use the 5Ps of voice (see Chapter 10) in your presentation

As it is a visual and audio medium, your slides will be more important than ever. Make your slides as interesting as possible. The following slide makes it much easier for the audience to absorb information than simply talking about the numbers.

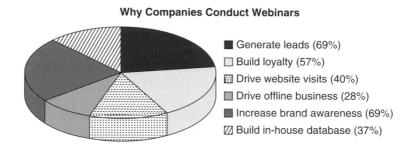

If video is being used, it is tempting to look at the screen instead of the camera and this can seem very odd to the audience. It is counter-intuitive to look into the camera, especially if you have notes, but it is very important in order to maintain rapport. Similarly, how you sit is important – being centred rather than off to one side, and not being too close to the screen, which can appear aggressive or imposing. Sitting too far away creates too much of a barrier with your audience and you lose a sense of intimacy. Distance may reduce the prominence of wrinkles or blemishes on screen but will reduce the quality of sound too.

The advantages of doing a webinar instead of a live event are significant:

- There are no venue costs so it is easier to provide a cost-effective way of delivering your webinar to your audience, passing on the cost savings to them or even doing them for free.

- There are no heavy equipment and materials to move around. When you are doing a presentation or running a training programme you have the laptop, cables, projector, handbooks and goodness knows what else to carry around. It can feel as though you are moving house!

- Geography is not a barrier to participation. This means that you can have participants from all over the world, thereby increasing your potential for audience numbers considerably.

- You can deliver your webinar in dressing gown and slippers if you want to as, unless you are using video, no one will see you. However, you also need to consider whether this will make you feel *too* relaxed. You want to make sure that you have the right mindset and energy level to deliver a professional presentation.

One final thing: as it is a webinar, you need to make sure you market it well and do the follow-up, otherwise you will be communicating into a vacuum and wasting a significant amount of your time.

VIDEO

The difference with video over a conventional type of presentation is that anyone can watch it and it exists beyond the life of your presentation – people can watch it in years to come so it is worth taking time to do it well.

In addition, you need to be mindful of what people can see – you don't have the luxury of walking around or using expansive body language to illustrate your points because it may not be captured on screen, unless you are being videoed by a professional. As you present you have to imagine yourself in a picture frame which means that your enthusiasm needs to be carried in more contained body language and in your voice.

Even though anyone can watch it, you still need to aim the video at your specific audience and the following questions apply:

1. Why are you doing the video?

2. Who is it aimed at?

3. What do they want/need?

COACH'S TIP

Remember who the video is aimed at

Always think about how you can project your brand values in your video – the personality of your business. Is it formal? Casual? Quirky?

Then consider how you want your audience to feel. Inspired? Thoughtful and reflective? Focused? Understood? This will help you to create the content and the tone.

If you decide on a do-it-yourself approach, here are some ideas for you:

- A flip camera is simple to use, portable, tripod-enabled and you can load video straight onto your computer afterwards.

- Lighting – make sure that you have three-point lighting: one either side of you at a 45° angles and one behind you so that you don't cast a shadow.

- Background – this should be clutter free. You don't want a bottle of wine to your left, an overstuffed in-tray to your right and chaos behind you.

- Do a sound-check to make sure you can be heard properly and make sure there are no outside noises to interfere with the quality.

- You can use a flipchart to the side of your video listing your main points if you need a low-tech teleprompt, but do make sure you look into the lens as much as possible – you don't want to look like you are reading. You should rehearse just as much as you would a conventional presentation so that the flipchart should not be a crutch.

- Keep it steady – use a tripod if you are doing this for yourself.

- The image should be at the right height and centred – you might need to do a few short image takes to get this right, though it is easier to get a friend to do this for you.

- Relax and look into the camera lens – imagine a good friend is smiling back at you.

- Wait a few moments before you speak and after you finish so the video doesn't seem to begin and end abruptly.

You may want to edit the video and put in an introduction and end slide with music to ease the viewer into and out of it.

Finally, think about how you will make it available – DVD, on your website or on YouTube.

SKYPE

Skype allows you to conduct video calls online and the principles are similar to doing a conventional video. You need to make sure that you are centred in your screen. Eye contact is tricky because it is natural to look into the screen, but to your audience this will look like you are looking down which can make you look quite shifty. Instead, look straight into the camera lens. Make sure your audio is working well so they can hear you properly and vice versa. To make your Skype call you will need:

- your computer with Skype loaded
- a web camera
- a microphone.

Do make sure you:

- always test audio and video before your presentation (found under 'Preferences')
- eliminate distracting noise
- set the lighting so that you can be seen by the other person (you will get an image of yourself to check this out)
- use headset and headphones to avoid echo.

RADIO

With radio it is very difficult to gain rapport with the audience so it is important to have rapport with your interviewer. Do make sure you listen to their show as part of your research so that you have a good understanding of the style of presentation, type of questions you might expect and whether or not the audience will interact with you. This will help you adopt the right mindset.

You will have to rely on your voice completely for audience rapport so make sure you adopt an appropriate tone to match your message.

Using the interviewer's name can also help to build rapport with your audience as it will make you come across as friendly.

Do rehearse the points you want to make in advance as the interviewer can take you off target. Use the politician's tactic: 'I think the important thing is ...' and make your intended point no matter what the question. Do use a respectful and kind tone so that you maintain rapport. If you have agreed the subject of your presentation in advance this should not be an issue but it is worth having this technique up your sleeve just in case.

Do make sure you remove any jangly jewellery as this can cause annoying punctuations to your message if you gesticulate. Also, make sure your mouth is the correct distance from the microphone and that you keep your head still, otherwise your voice will be zooming in and out.

Check whether you are allowed to take notes in with you and, if so, take care as the audience can hear you fiddling with your papers. Alternatively, have your interview notes on an electronic device that makes no sound at all.

Finally, if you are promoting your business, do remember to give details of how to contact you, i.e. your website address.

INVESTOR PRESENTATIONS

If you are a start-up, or you require an injection of capital, you may well be required to do a presentation to potential investors. These are people who are interested in one or both of the following:

- Making money through minimal effort
- The excitement of what is essentially a gamble.

Investors are typically very astute people and, while they may have an abundance of cash, they will be concerned about the level of risk.

It is therefore incumbent on you to assure them that you are as safe a bet as it's possible to be. How to do this? First and foremost it will be the level of confidence you have in your presentation. That will be a function of the level of knowledge and confidence you have in your business. Consider the following questions:

Do you come across as passionate?	Passion is contagious – if you are passionate, it will engender an air of excitement in your audience, assuming that you have all the other elements in balance.
Are you confident or arrogant?	Confidence is self-belief with humility – the willingness to admit if you are wrong and to listen to advice. Some investors will want to invest their finance and their expertise. They will want to contribute their advice *and* will expect you either to accept it or give them a very good reason why not. This needs to be done respectfully, especially if you are in the initial stages and you want to develop trust.
	Arrogance, on the other hand, is confidence with more than a hint of self-importance and superiority. Arrogant people are very difficult to work with and often exaggerate their achievements, abilities and potential. This does not engender trust – quite the opposite.
	If you are neither confident nor arrogant, this assumes that you do not have the belief in yourself, in your proposition, or both. Either way, it is unlikely that you will gain the investment you are looking for.

Do you know your numbers?	Investors are numbers people. Your business plan needs to reflect this. Are you familiar with your set-up costs? Do they stack up? What are your projections? Are they realistic? What are the assumptions you have made in your projections? If you are not clear on your numbers and able to talk about them fluently, this will create doubt and its twin, caution. Here are a few to be getting along with:
	<ul><li>Sales</li><li>Revenues</li><li>Cost of sales</li><li>Gross profit</li><li>Costs:<ul><li>Marketing and PR</li><li>Research and development</li><li>Manufacturing</li><li>Operations – HR, customer services, administration, finance, logistics, IT</li></ul></li><li>Selling price</li><li>Commission/margin to resellers</li><li>Rent, rates, equipment, furniture</li><li>Interest</li><li>Tax</li><li>Hiring costs</li><li>Legal and consultancy fees</li><li>Cash flow projections</li><li>Net income</li></ul>Most investors will expect to see a five-year plan.
Have you thought through the different elements of the project?	Investors will be looking to reduce any degree of risk. They want to know that the money they have invested is safe and that it will make a good return. So, the more you have thought through each aspect of the business plan, the more confidence you will instil in your proposition. Consider the following:<ul><li>The product/service you are providing</li><li>Target market</li><li>Your vision and mission</li></ul>

	• Is this a new investment or a follow-on?
	• Are you looking for one investor or several?
	• The amount required
	• Competitive analysis on specific features, service and the price
	• Marketing plan
	• Sales plan
	• Resourcing plan
	• Facilities and equipment
	• Research and development
	• Product details and specifications together with compatibility issues if appropriate
	• Risks and how to mitigate them
	• What, specifically, you plan to do with the money?
	• Why now?
	• What is the compelling reason?
Do you have credibility?	Credibility will be a function of how you present, blended with content and your credentials. What is your background relevant to this project? Your qualifications? Your experience? All of these, added to your voice, body language and appearance will either enhance or detract from your credibility. Time invested in all of these will pay off, in more ways than one.
	If you are working with others, do give a summary of your Executive Team – the people who are involved in the project. You will need to show that you have a rounded team, with a breadth and depth of skillset which will ensure a successful delivery of your proposition.
	Include testimonials as an endorsement of you, your product and/or your service.
	Put yourself in your potential investors' shoes: Would you be willing to sacrifice your children's university fund to your project?
	For information on how to build rapport and gravitas, see Chapter 10.

Do your homework and you will present with more confidence and deal with the barrage of questions you will be faced with more elegantly. You need to be able to drill down into the detail of the numbers, know them inside-out, as though you live them and breathe them.

At times, you will also need to do investor updates. These will be fun and enjoyable when you are on target and exceeding expectations. Who doesn't want to know that their investment yielded more than predicted?

However, as an entrepreneur, you will not be alone if your forecast was optimistic and the reality has fallen short. Here you need a blend of sensitivity and confidence. It is doubtful whether there is a single business that has not made a mistake – some more glaring than others. The problem is not in the mistake but in how it is dealt with. What your investor will need to see is a clear plan to get back on target and protect his investment. He will need confidence that you know why the problem happened, that you have a plan to get back on track and that plan is credible and achievable given the events that have preceded it.

They believed you before; you need to show that they can believe you again. Making bold statements without substance will not help, even if they are delivered with enthusiasm.

Make sure you have finished speaking before your audience has finished listening.

Dorothy Sarnoff

NEXT STEPS

In this chapter you have looked in more depth about the purposes and approaches to specific types of presentation. These include in-house presentations such as employee or departmental meetings as well as external presentations such as to clients and prospects. You have also looked in depth at how to do webinars, video, radio interviews, etc.

You have looked at how to consider how to structure your for different stakeholders, from the Managing Director to the IT Manager, The HR Manager and everything in between. You have even looked at what you need to consider if you are training to secure investment.

In the next chapter you will learn about a specific type of business presentation – the elevator pitch. This deserves a chapter on its own as this is a key area for most people in business.

👍 TAKEAWAYS

This is your opportunity to take stock of what you have learned from this chapter. You might want now to choose other chapters and exercises to focus on, or you can continue to work through the whole book if this fits your needs more.

Think of a business presentation you have seen in the past that you admired. What made it such a good presentation? Be very specific and think in terms of:

The presenter:

The content:

Style and structure:

Now think of a business presentation you have seen in the past that you did not enjoy. What was it about the presentation that caused you to judge it this way? Again, be specific and think in terms of:

The presenter:

The content:

Style and structure:

Bearing these examples in mind, what actions do you want to take when preparing your own presentations?

4 DEVELOPING YOUR ELEVATOR PITCH

✔ OUTCOMES FOR THIS CHAPTER:

- In this chapter we will learn how to develop your elevator pitch, look at the different types of pitch and discover a variety of ways to structure your own elevator pitch.

Most people are asked 'What do you do?' both in a business context and socially. In this chapter, we will explore how to conduct an effective elevator pitch which informs and which also inspires interest. It is called an elevator pitch because it is something you can say between floors when faced with someone asking you what it is that you do. It can make all the difference in winning a piece of business and never hearing from a person ever again.

If you are a regular networker, you are probably used to your 'minute to win-it', your '60 seconds', '40 seconds' or similar. But how effective is it? Do you have people asking for your business card, looking at the front and back of it and asking to put a meeting in the diary? Or do their eyes glaze over?

The elevator pitch is an essential part of your networking and marketing strategy. As well as being a showcase for what you do, it is also a referral generator – inspiring people to recommend you to others, thereby building your business profile and your profits.

It has the power to develop, or undermine, the know–like–trust concept. If people know you, like you and trust you, they are more likely to refer business to you rather than to someone else in your field.

The typical structure for an elevator pitch is as follows:

Your name
Your business name (and/or something attention-grabbing)
What you do
Who you do it for
What kind of referrals you are looking for (if you are at a networking event) or some other call to action
Your name
Your business name
A memorable strapline

Here is an example:

I am Jennifer Gleeson
My business is Gleeson Graphics
We design business graphics which create a positive impression for your business
We do this for small companies in the service industry
I am looking for referrals from businesses that want to refresh their brochures, business cards and websites so that they stand out from the crowd
I'm Jennifer Gleeson
Gleeson Graphics
Creating the right impression for your business

To be effective it needs to inspire and motivate. That, of course, will be highly reliant on your delivery.

You may also include any of the following:

- **Update people about the effect of recent news** For an accountant, any news about the economy can create good content for their pitch. For example, 'Now we are working our way out of recession, it is the perfect time to look at what you can do to reduce your costs and maximize your profits.'

- **An interesting statistic** For a garage: 'There may have been 34,000 cars produced so far this year, but we are only interested in yours. We want to make sure that your car is working as well as it did when it first came off the production line.'

- **An announcement about a new product or service** For a beautician: 'For years we have offered the latest in natural skin care. We are proud to announce the latest in natural wrinkle reduction – no needles, no poison, just natural good looks from Amazing Skin.'

- **A mini case study** For a travel consultant: 'We recently helped to create the holiday of their dreams for a young couple going on honeymoon. She wanted a beach holiday and he wanted a safari. We have combined a two-centre holiday so they get the best of both worlds. They are thrilled. Marriage is a journey of compromise, but not of quality.'

- **Something topical, such as relating to the season or the date** For a catering company: 'With summer in full swing, we want to help you enjoy outdoor entertaining without being chained to the BBQ – we offer delicious, elegant and affordable outdoor dining so you can enjoy the company of your guests and this glorious sunshine.'

- **A current project you are working on** For a garden designer: 'We are currently working on a courtyard garden for a small cottage. It will be low maintenance, with a zen theme and year-round colour so that the owner can enjoy this outdoor room for relaxation and entertaining.'

- **A prop** For a virtual assistant: 'Here is a box. Inside is all the paperwork my new client has collected over the past year. My job is to sift through it, throw away rubbish, create an easy-to-use filing system and customer database, and do his expenses for him. I do all the jobs you hate so that you can spend more time doing the jobs you love.'

When putting together your elevator pitch, consider the following questions:

- **Who are you helping?** It pays to be specific about your target audience so that your pitch resonates with the right people. Saying 'anyone' can really dilute your message – though it is mightily tempting to do!

- **What problem are you solving?** Most people who are in business are solving some kind of problem. Using the examples of businesses above, these are:

    - Accountant – how to meet statutory requirements, save money, increase profits
    - Garage – fixing a damaged or faulty car
    - Travel consultant – where to go on holiday that meets your criteria
    - Beautician – calming blemished skin or slowing the signs of ageing
    - Caterer – for people who want to entertain but don't have the time
    - Garden designer – lack of vision but a love of gardens
    - Virtual assistant – too much work and not enough time

- **What benefit are you increasing?** Are you improving the speed of something? The look of something? The quality of something? The effect of something? Is there a return on their investment? Will profits be increased? Self-esteem? Kudos? Lifespan? Customer satisfaction? The list goes on. Think of what you are able to improve and expand on it. Be playful, take your time. It is surprising, when you brainstorm, how many possibilities come to mind.

- **How much are you saving?** You've considered the benefits, but now you need to think about what is being saved. Is it money? Is it time? Perhaps it is stress? Or paper? Or the ozone layer? Again, be playful and see what you come up with.

- **What are you saving them from?** This is a catch-all question. Are you saving them from themselves? From legal action? From failure? From the competition?

Now it's time for you to have a go:

COACHING SESSION 3

Elevator pitch

What could you include to get people's attention?

What project or case study could you talk about which would position you as expert in your field?

What is topical at the moment which you could use in your elevator pitch?

Brainstorm some memorable straplines:

If you are putting together your elevator pitch, you may want to think about whether to vary your presentation or repeat it. There is no hard-and-fast rule, but here are some of the benefits of each:

	Repeat	Vary
Benefits	Creates familiarity with your message Makes it memorable	Enables you to show the breadth of what you do Enables you to be topical
Disadvantages	May become boring May lack breadth and scope	It may confuse It may have less power

You might want to consider having six different messages that you rotate. This enables you to get the best of both worlds and means you don't have to spend so much time thinking about what to say each time as you would with the 'vary' option.

While crafting your elevator pitch causes you to focus on the words you use, actually the words only account for about 7 per cent of how your message is perceived. Body language, by comparison, accounts for about 55 per cent. And what about the other 38 per cent? That comes from your voice.

So, what does this mean? It means that, as well as crafting your 60 seconds with economy of words – saying what you need to say in as few words as possible – you need to think about how you say it. If you are slumped and downcast but using words of enthusiasm, they will believe your body language every time.

COACH'S TIP

Body language

If your voice and your body language are at odds, your body language will win out.

Consider the following: 'We are the best computer support company in the area.' Those words are pretty good, aren't they? If you had a problem with your computer, wouldn't you want to go to the best? Of course you would.

However, if there is no energy in your voice and you do not have eye contact with the audience, what will they make of your message?

In your pitch, unless you are a funeral director, you need to bring energy and enthusiasm to your presentation. Add to that conviction and you have a winning formula.

If you are a therapist, you may choose a gentler tone, but you still want your passion in your work to shine through.

Other tips for an effective pitch include:

- **Avoid the antipodean lift** There is a growing tendency for people to lift the end of their sentences so that statements are heard as questions. This creates doubt in your message. Let's take the following two examples:

    - We are the best website developers in the area? (upward lift)

    - We are the best website developers in the area. (ending on a low note)

    Which one is more believable?

- **Avoid the bored or unconfident wither** This is where the voice trails off before it gets to the end as though you have run out of steam. It is almost impossible to have any credibility in your message if you don't have conviction in your voice. So, it's important to maintain a level of energy in your voice so that your message is carried with it.

- **Use positive body language** Your body language needs to support your message. Your shoulders need to be relaxed, your eyes connecting with the audience and a relaxed expression on your face.

- **Avoid jargon and acronyms** You don't want anything to stand in the way of people understanding what you're talking about.

- **Talk about benefits, not features** (See Chapter 10 for more information.) Here are some more examples for specific professions:

    - I am a dentist – I give people beautiful smiles.

    - I write databases – I double the value of your data.

- I sell cars – I make your time on the road more enjoyable, safer and more economical.

■ **Let them know your ideal referral** When you are specific, it triggers a much more focused response in your audience. If you hear 'I want referrals from sales people', your mind might not engage with the generality of the statement. However, if you were to hear 'I am looking for sales people who would like more quality leads' you are more likely to get what you want.

A MORE POWERFUL START

We have already outlined the conventional approach to your elevator pitch. A more impactful one might be to start with a fact or a controversial statement. If you are going to early morning networking events, this can liven up your audience who will often be sleepy and bored.

So, instead of starting with 'Hello, I am Freddie Dreamer and I sell high-quality beds', you might want to say, 'Sixty per cent of people have trouble sleeping. Sleep is when your mind and body replenish themselves. If you aren't sleeping well, you aren't functioning well. My name is Freddie Dreamer and I am in the business of helping you sleep well. We produce high quality beds …'.

This can really get people's attention and make them sit up.

STORIES THAT SELL

A powerful way of making your pitch is through a story. All good stories have a villain, a victim and a hero. It is possible to adapt this concept for the purpose of promoting your business. For example, for HR company HR Associates it might look something like this:

The teaser	You never know when something good will turn out bad.
The intro	My name is Steve Campbell, from Your HR Associates.
The story	My client had a problem with a member of staff who ticked all the boxes – great experience with a good company and who came across very well at interview. It all started so well but soon the cracks appeared and the employee started to be surly towards customers, got sloppy with his orders and was creating problems with staff. They called me in to see what could be done about it. The staff member is now on a performance improvement plan and is progressing nicely. We are monitoring this to ensure it stays that way.
The call to action	I am looking for referrals to companies with more than ten staff in the Surrey area.
Close	My name is Steve Campbell, from Your HR Associates.
Memorable strapline	Big enough to cope, small enough to care.

Clearly, the client is the 'victim', the employee 'the villain' and Steve is the 'hero'.

COACH'S TIP

Tell a story

Stories are a good way of illustrating what you do in a compelling way.

THE MESSAGE MAP APPROACH

Another way to approach your pitch is to produce a message map. This is very simple to do and is particularly helpful if you have a complicated offering. First of all you create a bite-size heading.

Then, create three main aspects of your business to develop the concept.

Then, develop those three aspects further. For example, for cake-making company Charlotte's Cakes it might look something like this:

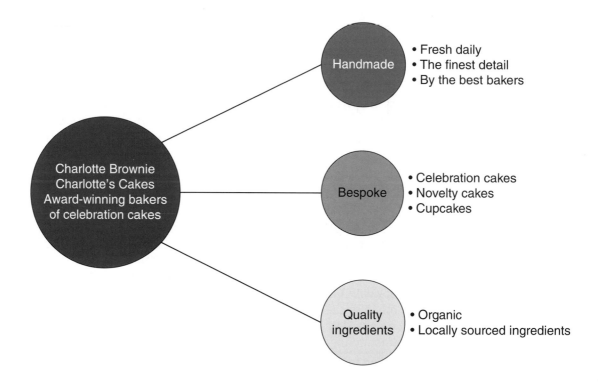

This gives you three possible presentations, depending on the amount of time you have available:

1. 'Hello, I am Charlotte Brownie of Charlotte's Cakes and we are an award-winning baker of celebration cakes.'

2. 'Hello, I am Charlotte Brownie of Charlotte's Cakes. We are an award-winning baker of celebration cakes which are handmade, bespoke and use only the finest ingredients.'

3. 'Hello, I am Charlotte Brownie of Charlotte's Cakes. We are an award-winning baker of celebration cakes. They are handmade daily with great attention to detail by the best bakers. They are bespoke, ranging from celebration cakes to novelty cakes and cupcakes. We use only the finest ingredients which are 70 per cent organic and locally sourced.'

The message map is great way to develop various options of presenting your message depending on the time available to you.

> *Your attitude precedes you. You make a statement long before you open your mouth.*
>
> Nicholas Boothman

→ NEXT STEPS

In this chapter you have looked at different approaches for how to do an elevator pitch so that you can make a strong and positive impact in a very short space of time. This is essential for most people in business.

You have looked at different examples for content that makes a presentation compelling and what to consider when you are putting together your pitch. This includes the kind of people you are helping, what problem you are solving and more.

In the next chapter you will explore the different types of social presentation and how to do those effectively.

TAKEAWAYS

This is your opportunity to take stock of what you have learned from this chapter. You might want now to choose other chapters and exercises to focus on, or you can continue to work through the whole book if this fits your needs more.

What memorable elevator pitches have you heard?

What made them memorable?

Given the examples above, which style of elevator pitch appeals to you the most?

Write your elevator pitch here. Practise so that you can speak with confidence. If you practise in front of a mirror you can see how you come across. Time it so that you can say everything within the allocated time. You don't want to be cut off before your strapline and you don't want to rush it either.

SOCIAL SPEAKING

- In this chapter we will consider the different types of social speeches including wedding speeches, eulogies and thank yous. We will look at what is required in each case, and some useful example are given to help you structure your own social speech.

In Chapter 2 we looked at the different types of speech. In this chapter we will be looking at social speeches specifically. These are less formal than business speeches. You don't need to worry about office politics or hecklers (apart from the good-natured banter). So, in many ways, the social speech is much easier and more enjoyable.

However, they still carry with them the same level of fear and trepidation of having to stand up in front of an audience, with a sense of responsibility to make it interesting and entertaining which only increases the nerves.

WEDDING SPEECHES

These have more scope for fun and mischief than other social speeches. Apart from the father of the bride, the groom and the best man, it is becoming more common for brides to want to have their moment too, and why not?

The best man has the added pressure of being awarded this role and entrusted to do a sterling job.

Conventionally, the speeches are general conducted after the meal in the following order:

- Father of the bride
- Groom
- Bride (if she wants to)
- Best man.

In terms of content, the following guidelines apply.

Father of the bride

Debrett's, the authority on etiquette, recommend that the father of the bride should:

- thank the guests for coming
- thank those involved with organizing the wedding
- tell some stories and affectionate anecdotes about the bride
- compliment the bride on how she looks
- welcome the groom to the family
- make a toast to 'the bride and groom'.

Here is an example of a father-of-the bride speech:

I thank you all for coming here to share this special day with us.

Arranging this wedding has been a real team effort – Angie and James have been brilliant, as have James's parents. The team at the hotel have been exemplary and Lexie, the chief bridesmaid, has been a tremendous support in putting all of this together too. This has meant that what could have been a stressful time has actually been a pleasure to organize as it has helped to deepen the bonds between our families.

When I got married to Joan, it was the happiest day of my life. And then my beautiful Angie came along and it changed everything. I didn't know it was possible to love so much and we have been gifted with a beautiful, kind and talented daughter. Nothing can prepare for you for a love like that.

She has been a model daughter to us both. She did so well at school, made good friends, loved dancing and was an excellent tennis player. The only time she gave us sleepless nights was when she started having boyfriends!

As a father I was incredibly protective and was really worried about the boys she would bring home. They were big on tattoos and nose-studs but short on conversation and eye contact. It was an anxious time for Joan and me. We started to despair that there would not be anyone good enough for our little girl but we bit our tongues and crossed our fingers.

Then one day she brought home James. A full body check revealed not a single piercing and only the smallest tattoo (on his right ankle below the sock line). But more important than that, he was attentive, respectful and has slotted right into our family. Very quickly he became like the son we never had and we couldn't be happier.

As a couple, they are considerate, loving and respectful to one another. They have shown that they understand the importance of compromise. These form the cornerstones of a good marriage. We can see that Angie is completely in love with him and it is obvious he feels the same way. As a parent, you cannot ask for more. I know they are planning a family and they will both make exceptional parents.

Angie is now making a life with James and, if they are half as happy as Joan and I have been, they will be very lucky indeed.

Angie has never looked more beautiful or more happy.

Please raise your glasses to Angie and James.

Groom

Debrett's advises that the groom's speech should:

- thank the father of the bride (or equivalent) on behalf of himself and his new wife for the speech
- thank the guests for coming
- thank the bride's parents if they are hosting the wedding
- thank his parents for raising him
- thank the best man for supporting him
- thank anyone who has helped in the planning of the wedding
- present both mothers (if applicable) with bouquets
- compliment his bride on how beautiful she is
- make a toast to 'the bridesmaids'.

At his wedding, Tom Fletcher of the band McFly confessed that the only anxiety he had about the wedding was the speech, because of his fear of public speaking. Declaring that this dread was because he didn't know how to write a good speech but he could write a good song, he then took a couple of their big hits and changed the words to suit the occasion. You can watch it using this link: http://www.youtube.co./watch?v=27WufdasQYs

He made it very personal so that everyone mentioned had a little anecdote about them. There were tears, jokes, a mild flirtation with his new sister-in-law, audience participation and even a choir.

It lasts nearly 15 minutes and has clearly taken a lot of thought to put together. However, your speech need only be a few minutes and you don't need the choir, guitar or piano unless you really want to push the boat out.

Tom injects a good dose of humour and humility. It is both heart-warming and amusing and is worth watching for some inspiration.

Best man

For a best man's speech, according to Debrett's, the following are the areas to cover:

- Reading out messages from people who could not attend, including emails.
- A selection of stories and anecdotes about the groom.
- Reveal something light-hearted and fun that will embarrass the groom.
- Some stories about the couple, how they met, their relationship and a few compliments for the bride.
- The tone should be witty and amusing rather than shocking or smutty.
- It should finish with a toast 'to Mr and Mrs (surname)'.

References to trees, handcuffs and a trouser-less groom are often used for comedic effect but always be mindful of your audience.

For a good example of a best man's speech, where the best man uses warmth and humour, stumbles across his words as most best men do, thereby making it real and natural, you may enjoy this one for inspiration. It is delightful in its informality: http://www.youtube.com/watch?v=7YWMVXh-wFs

Preparation is key for these speeches, as always. And it's a good idea not to have too much to drink beforehand as it can disinhibit you and cause you to say things you might regret in the morning. Since most speeches are now videoed this means that any slurring or inappropriate remarks are captured for evermore. Not only that, it may even make its way onto YouTube.

 COACH'S TIP

Preparation

Preparation is key to making a good speech – thinking about your audience, deciding what you want to say and how, as well as having lots of practice.

When you prepare your speech it helps to type it onto A5 cards with one sentence per line and large spaces between lines. This makes it easier to read and helps you make eye contact with the audience.

In practising the speech, do stand up and read it out loud, making sure there is variety in your voice. Think in terms of the 5Ps:

Pace This is the speed at which you speak. Too fast and people won't be able to keep up. Too slow and you will send them off to sleep – especially if they have had a drink or two. You can also change pace within the speech. If you are talking about something sentimental, you may want to slow your voice down. If you are delivering a punchline to a joke, you may want to speed it up.

Pitch This is the quality of the sound of your voice, the rise and fall of the tone and the volume. Again, variety is important.

Also, think about whether you want certain words to stand out. You can do this easily with your voice tone (and the pause – see below). For example, try reading out the following sentence by emphasizing different parts of it each time you repeat it. Notice how it changes the meaning of the sentence completely:

1. **I** am the best man.

2. I **am** the best man.

3. I am **the** best man.

4. I am the **best** man.

5. I am the best **man**.

In example 1, it is indicating that perhaps there had been some question as to who was the best man. It is an answer to the question 'Who is the best man?'

In example 2, it insinuates that he is affirming his role as though he doubted himself at first or that someone else doubted it.

In example 3, it suggests that there is no best man better than him in the history of time.

In example 4, he is implying that, of all the men, he is the best one.

In example 5, he is saying that, among all the men, he is the best but there may be a woman who is better than him.

Projection Projection refers to the power of your voice, not the volume. A useful trick is to imagine projecting your voice into the next room. Using this technique will usually cause your voice to land comfortably in your audience.

Pause Pauses are really important to help people absorb your message and in providing punctuation.

Consider the effect of the following sentences – the first without pauses and the second with pauses:

1. I met the groom when he was only five years old he was insufferably attention-seeking and had a habit of eating my sandwiches in preference to his own despite these obvious character flaws he was popular with the girls and the funniest boy at school he was clever too to say I was jealous would be an understatement.

2. I met the groom when he was only five years old ... He was insufferably attention-seeking ... and he had a habit of eating my sandwiches in preference to his own ... Despite these obvious character flaws he was popular with the girls and the funniest boy at school ... He was clever too ... To say I was jealous would be an understatement.

The second example provides the space for your points to be made and absorbed by the audience.

Pauses are also important if you are delivering a punchline to a joke – you will get a much better laugh.

Precision Precision is about how clearly you articulate your words. If you have had a few drinks, it can really interfere with your delivery and people may not be able to decipher your slurred speech. In Chapter 10, there are some tongue-twisters to help you develop your ability to articulate words effectively.

COACH'S TIP

The 5Ps

Using the 5Ps will enable you to make the best impact and your speech will become a highlight.

IS IT OK TO READ YOUR SPEECH?

Yes. Even presidents and prime ministers read their speeches. They have just learned to do it while maintaining good eye contact and flow. Writing only one main point on a card and one sentence a line is effective in helping you do this. It helps you to make eye contact with the audience. They will think you're a professional.

Generally, A5 cards are easier to use than typed A4 paper – it will be less obvious if you are shaking and you will not be overwhelmed by the amount of text on the page.

COACHING SESSION 4

The more practice you have, the more confident you will be. Practise standing up as this will emulate how you will deliver the speech on the day. If you can, record the speech and critique it. Consider the following questions and make some notes on how you could improve.

1. Is it clear?

2. Does it flow?

3. Is there a variety in tone and pace?

4. Do you use pauses well?

5. Is there precision in your speech?

6. Does it entertain?

7. Is it likely to hurt anyone's feelings?

8. Might anyone be offended by it?

9. Is it too long or too short?

10. Will people enjoy it?

Practise and refine. Practise and refine. Practise and refine.

WHAT IF YOU MAKE A MISTAKE ON THE DAY?

It is not the end of the world to make a mistake or lose your place, or stumble on a word. If you do, just laugh and the audience will laugh with you. You could use a one-liner such as 'I'm glad I made a mistake. It was going too well and I really don't like smug people.' You will find that the audience will warm to you if you are humble but they will feel sorry for you if you appear crestfallen.

EULOGIES

Eulogies can be very difficult to write – deciding how to set the right tone in front of people who are bereaved and emotional, and how to pay respects to your loved one in a way they would appreciate, requires care and sensitivity.

Some people prefer to read out a poem (see some examples below). However, it is more personal if you write a speech from the heart. Perhaps include some anecdotes about the deceased, something about them as a person, what they loved, how they lived their life, an amusing story and perhaps something that they taught you. Its purpose is to create a portrait of the deceased and to honour them.

Here is an example:

My father was first and foremost a family man. The youngest of five, he lost his mother when he was four and it is perhaps for this reason that he lived for his family and worked three jobs to provide for us all.

One of his great pleasures was playing the piano. He was self-taught and was so thrilled when we showed our appreciation, though he was only marginally better than Les Dawson! It was hugely endearing to watch him play.

He also loved to work in his garden, in which he took great pride, and in which there was many a family meal enjoyed. He was so passionate about it being just right and I remember that, in his eighties, when most people are taking it easy, he uprooted a whole tree-stump singlehandedly because it spoilt the view of his beloved roses.

My relationship with my father was not always easy – he was incredibly protective which caused some challenges. Yet I realize how similar we are and what he had taught me throughout his life.

We both have a bit of a temper which I now realize stems from his strong sense of right and wrong – a family trait which preceded him and which lives on. He also taught me about the importance of family – to love and forgive in equal measure.

He gave me – and my siblings – a strong work ethic. He worked so hard to provide for us throughout his life so that we had everything we could want or need. He instilled that work ethic into each of us. He was completely tireless. When he finished working, he would come home to work on one of his DIY projects to make our house a home.

He was incredibly loyal and would do anything for anyone. Sometimes I worried that he was being taken advantage of but he never saw it that way – he just wanted to give and took great pleasure in it.

I inherited his sense of humour which leaves some people bemused and others charmed and it is a trait that helped him through the numerous challenges he faced in his life.

He also taught me about the pleasures of food and wine and he loved nothing better than to have people over for dinner and regale them with his many stories.

In the last year of his life he became quite ill but bore his illness with humour, courage and good grace. He was a force of nature and will be missed so much.

You will see that this is providing mostly positive information, but is also honest in dealing with a negative quality in the speaker's father, which is delivered with sensitivity.

COACH'S TIP

Stories

People love stories, so do feel free to pick out some of the main points and illustrate them with a story.

It is best to use a conversational tone as it makes it more personal. It is OK to get emotional too. Just make sure you have some tissues to hand and perhaps a glass of water. Take a deep breath to compose yourself and continue when you can. Everybody will be on your side.

If you prefer to read out a poem instead, here are a few popular ones:

His Journey's Just Begun

Don't think of him as gone away
His journey's just begun
Life holds so many facets
This earth is only one.

Just think of him as resting
From the sorrows and the tears
In a place of warmth and comfort
Where there are no days and years.

Think how he must be wishing
That we could know today
How nothing but our sadness
Can really pass away.

And think of him as living
In the hearts of those he touched
For nothing loved is ever lost
And he was loved so much

Ellen Brenneman

Miss Me But Let Me Go

When I come to the end of the road
And the sun has set on me
I want no rites in a gloom filled room,
Why cry for a soul set free?

Miss me a little – but not for too long,
And not with your head bowed low.
Remember the love we once shared.
Miss me a little – but let me go.

For this is a journey that we all must take
And each must go alone.
It's all part of the Master's Plan
A step on the road to home.

When you are lonely and sick of heart,
Go to the friends we know
And bury your sorrows in doing good deeds.
Miss me – but let me go.

Anonymous

> **Do Not Stand At My Grave and Weep**
>
> Do not stand at my grave and weep,
>
> I am not there, I do not sleep,
>
> I am a thousand winds that blow
>
> I am the diamond glints of snow
>
> I am the sunlight on ripened grain
>
> I am the gentle Autumn rain.
>
> When you awaken in the morning's hush
>
> I am the swift uplifting rush
>
> Of quiet birds in circled flight
>
> I am the soft stars that shine at night
>
> Do not stand at my grave and cry
>
> I am not there. I did not die.
>
> Mary Elizabeth Frye

THANK YOUS

A thank-you speech may be something you are expecting to give, either to thank someone publicly for their help, or in response to being given a leaving present when it is tradition to do so. Or the need may occur spontaneously. This happens mostly if you have organized an event and someone takes it upon themselves to thank you for doing so. While this is spontaneous, it can also be anticipated. If you have any inkling that one may be required, it is better to plan it in advance if you can.

Always be gracious, warm and sincere. Thank you speeches are normally brief but do remember to thank people who have been supportive of you, as a success is usually a team-effort.

For an example of a thank you speech, do watch the video below. It actually contains two thank yous. It features Russell Crowe receiving his Oscar, and has the compere, Steve Martin, giving an amusing introduction to Hilary Swank, who presents the award to Crowe. Also interesting in this clip is that, following the usual thank yous, Crowe speaks movingly to those with 'childhood imaginings' on the 'downside of advantage, relying purely on courage'. View it at: http://www.youtube.com/watch?v=hwjqlN3jueg

The little voice in the back of your head will always find something wrong with you. But nobody else can hear that voice.

Unknown

NEXT STEPS

In this chapter you have looked at the different types of social presentations, or speeches, which you may be called upon to do. These vary from wedding speeches (groom, best man, father of the bride, and even the bride herself). You have seen what Debrett's (the authority on etiquette) recommend for each.

You have learned about the 5Ps of voice – Pace, Pitch, Projection, Pause and Precision.

You have also looked at how to do a eulogy and a thank-you speech and been shown various examples as an example of to follow.

In the next chapter you will look in more depth about the importance of knowing your audience so that your presentation has the most positive impact on them.

TAKEAWAYS

This is your opportunity to take stock of what you have learned from this chapter. You might want now to choose other chapters and exercises to focus on, or you can continue to work through the whole book if this fits your needs more.

What is a memorable social speech you have heard?

What made it memorable?

Think of a social speech you have made in the past. Given what you have learned in this chapter and in your example given above, how might you have done it differently to have an even bigger impact?

6 WHAT EVERY PRESENTER SHOULD KNOW

OUTCOMES FROM THIS CHAPTER

- In this chapter we will look at why you need to understand your audience before you start working on your presentation and the various mindsets your audience may have which could influence how you structure your presentation. We will also consider the questions you need to ask yourself so that you aren't blindsided.

In order to make the very best impression in your presentation, it is important to consider your audience. What are their problems, their needs, their expectations and their hidden agendas? When you have that level of insight, you can more easily tailor your presentation to have the best impact, whether you want to educate, entertain, sell or inform.

When you structure your presentation to address the specific needs of your audience effectively, you increase audience engagement and the ability to positively influence them to a specific outcome.

Remember that your audience is made up of individuals, so they will not all have the same level of knowledge of your subject. They will differ in their degree of friendliness or hostility, and will each be convinced in different ways: some will be more logical, some more emotional. They will have different hot buttons.

COACH'S TIP

Know your audience

Where possible, try to understand your audience before you start: what they already know; how they are likely to be feeling; your key supporters and detractors and their likely objections.

So, let's take a more in-depth look at how to get to know your audience.

WHAT PROBLEMS DO THEY FACE?

In making your presentation, it is essential to think about what problems your audience members might be facing. These can be specific to your presentation or more general.

Specific

How will your audience be feeling towards your presentation? The hope is always that your audience are open, willing and receptive. They have no axe to grind, no hidden agendas and are completely supportive and non-judgemental. That will make your presentation nice and easy. However, we are not always so lucky, so it's helpful to consider what negatives you may encounter so that you can prepare your message accordingly. What are the specific problems your audience face relative to your presentation? Will this cause them to be hostile? Or indifferent? Or could they be expecting some good news when what you will be delivering is bad news?

You might want to consider the possibilities along the following continuum:

Hostile			Indifferent			Receptive			Unsuspecting		
1	2	3	4	5	6	7	8	9	9	8	7

There are many variables as to how these might translate into actual examples, but here are some to help illustrate these for you:

- **Indifferent** The trainer who could be faced with delegates who have been forced to attend, so they may be grumpy and unwilling and thinking about all the 'real' work they should be getting on with.

- **Unsuspecting** The salesperson who already knows that his prospect is ready to buy and that the market leader has preceded him and that his prices are not very competitive. His audience are both hyped and expectant.

- **Unsuspecting into Hostile** The HR Director tasked with making some redundancies will encounter an unsuspecting audience who turn fearful, suspicious and perhaps angry.

- **Hostile or Indifferent** The manager who is implementing a new system to a change-resistant workforce is likely to experience resistance and apathy.

- **Hostile** The team member who is seen as the favourite may be met with heckling so that he is humiliated in front of his adoring boss.

- **Receptive** The boss who is about to introduce a long-awaited bonus scheme to his staff which will see a significant uplift in their overall earnings.

- **Hostile** The entrepreneur who is looking for investment. If some of the reactions on *Dragons' Den* are to be believed, his audience may be cynical, critical and intimidating.

General

How might your audience be feeling irrespective of the content of your presentation? Consider the following possibilities:

- Your presentation might be the first on the agenda, after the audience has experienced a tortuous journey to the venue. They might feel irritated or stressed and perhaps tired. Your presentation will need to bear this in mind, perhaps with an acknowledgement or just easing them into how you want them to feel.

- Your presentation might follow a highly motivational speaker and you are talking about cost management. You need to think carefully about how to maintain a positive energy with a potentially dull subject, without losing credibility. Not impossible, but it does need thought.

- If your presentation is after lunch – the so-called 'graveyard slot' – your audience is likely to be feeling drowsy after a carb-fuelled meal and it will be your job to bring them back to the here and now, feeling energized and engaged. A monotone voice with lots of detailed slides will tip them into a stupefied slumber.

HOW MUCH DO THEY KNOW?

In creating your presentation, do consider the current level of knowledge of your audience so that you don't patronize them or bore them with information they are already very familiar with.

HOW DO THEY FEEL ABOUT YOU?

Do the audience know you? Do they like you? Are they fearful of you? Do they resent you? Knowing how they feel about you will help you to pitch your presentation appropriately.

If they are fearful of you and you want to elicit input from them, it is unlikely you will get any useful information – you are only likely to hear what they think you want to hear, rather than the truth. So, it's important to make them feel safe. In Chapter 10 we talk about how to come across as approachable versus credible.

WHO ARE YOUR KEY INFLUENCERS AND DETRACTORS?

You also need to think about who your key influencers might be because they are the ones you need to support you. At the same time, who might your key detractors be?

COACH'S TIP

Detractors

Consider what you can do to win round your detractors, or at least minimize the level of disruption they might cause.

HOW ARE THEY LIKELY TO RESPOND TO YOUR MESSAGE?

In putting together your message think about what the likely objections of the audience might be, what might surprise them (negatively or positively), and what will they agree with.

Understanding is a two-way street.

Eleanor Roosevelt

NEXT STEPS

In this chapter, you have looked at the importance of understanding your audience. You have learned that by putting yourself in their shoes, you are better able to influence them to the outcome you want so that you are not taken by surprise at their reactions.

You have seen that there are various mindsets that your audience may present with which are either specific to your presentation (such as being open to the subject, indifferent to it or hostile towards it); or general, such as the timing of your presentation.

You have also seen the importance of understanding that how much they already know will impact how and what you present to them.

In the next chapter you will learn about how to structure your presentation and how to generate ideas for your content.

TAKEAWAYS

This is your opportunity to take stock of what you have learned from this chapter. You might want now to choose other chapters and exercises to focus on, or you can continue to work through the whole book if this fits your needs more.

How much does your audience already know?

How might your audience be feeling before you present?

How would you like your audience to feel during and after your presentation?

Who are your key influencers?

Who are your key supporters?

Who are your key detractors?

What are their hot buttons?

What are their likely objections?

What are they likely to approve of?

7 GETTING THE STRUCTURE AND CONTENT RIGHT

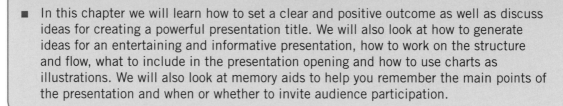

 OUTCOMES FOR THIS CHAPTER

- In this chapter we will learn how to set a clear and positive outcome as well as discuss ideas for creating a powerful presentation title. We will also look at how to generate ideas for an entertaining and informative presentation, how to work on the structure and flow, what to include in the presentation opening and how to use charts as illustrations. We will also look at memory aids to help you remember the main points of the presentation and when or whether to invite audience participation.

The amount of time you spend in preparing your presentation will depend on how high the stakes are. According to Nancy Duarte, author of *Slide:ology* and the person who created the presentation for Al Gore's award-winning film *An Inconvenient Truth* (2006), it takes between 36 and 90 hours to prepare a one-hour presentation with 30 slides. The stronger the risk factor, the more preparation you need.

In addition, people tend to forget 40 per cent of what is said within 20 minutes of your presentation. According to Shay McConnon in his book *Presenting with Power*, within half a day, they will lose 60 per cent of your message and, by the time one week has passed, 90 per cent of your message will have been forgotten. This has a huge impact on how you design and deliver your presentation.

As Steven Covey said, 'Begin with the end in mind'. Knowing what you want to communicate, why it's important and what you want to have happen as a result is critical to the success of your presentation. This will inform the structure and content which we will deal with later on in the chapter.

SETTING A CLEAR OUTCOME

COACH'S TIP

Know where you are going

A clear outcome will help you to achieve your objectives more easily.

An outcome is a result you are seeking to achieve from your presentation. Some common outcomes are to:

- inform
- inspire
- teach
- explain
- reassure
- get commitment to an idea
- gain support for a cause
- win a sale
- change thinking
- elicit input.

Whether you have an audience of one or many, it is essential that you consider what, as a result of your presentation, you want them to:

- do
- change
- think
- feel
- understand
- commit to.

COACHING SESSION 5

Presentation outcome

Think of an upcoming presentation and complete the following sentence:

At the end of my presentation, I would like my audience to:

COACH'S TIP

Target your focus

Focus on what you *do* want, rather than what you *don't* want – remember always to state it in the positive.

Here are some examples of positive outcomes:

1. At the end of my presentation, I would like my audience to feel excited about our service and sign up to a twelve-month contract (feel, do).

2. At the end of my presentation, I would like my audience to commit to producing a weekly report and think about how to implement it (commit, think).

3. At the end of my presentation, I would like my audience to understand and adopt the new call-handling technology to reduce wait times (understand, change).

4. At the end of my presentation, I would like my audience to understand the new restructure, what it means to them and to feel excited about it (understand, feel).

5. At the end of my presentation, I would like my audience to commit to a 10 per cent increase in headcount and consider what they need to do to accommodate it (commit, think).

6. At the end of my presentation, I would like my audience to understand the new order processing software and to start using it (understand, do).

7. At the end of my presentation, I would like my audience to support my department in a more collaborative way, being more appreciative of its needs (change, think).

8. At the end of my presentation, I would like my audience to understand the difference between results and projections and gain a commitment from each department to get back on track (understand, commit).

Injecting feeling

In Chapter 3, there is an illustration showing why companies conduct webinars. If you were to think of an outcome that could be used for this slide, assuming it is part of a wider presentation to teach webinar skills, it might be:

- **Example 1** At the end of the presentation, I want my audience to understand webinars, their benefits, their limitations, and how to construct an effective and persuasive webinar with confidence and enthusiasm.

You will notice that there are a couple of 'feeling' words in there – 'confidence' and 'enthusiasm'. It is useful to think about how you want your audience to feel as a result of the presentation. Here is why. Compare example 1 to example 2:

- **Example 2** At the end of the presentation, I want my audience to understand webinars, their benefits, their limitations, and how to construct an effective and persuasive webinar.

Without the 'confidence and enthusiasm' to guide you, it is easy to forget these as you prepare your presentation. The result is the risk of a less interesting and, worse, a boring presentation. The result could be a failure to create the level of interest in your audience producing their own webinars – the core purpose of your presentation. Example 2 is a basic outcome, whereas Example 1 has a deeper meaning to it. When you include the emotions in the outcome, it forces the mind to think of ways to engender those emotions in the content and style of your presentation. It is a way of focusing your mind and actions towards the most positive outcome for you.

COACHING SESSION 6

Modify your outcome

Modify the outcome you have already created to reflect how you want the audience to feel during and/or following your presentation:

At the end of my presentation, I would like my audience to feel:

The importance of a positively stated outcome can't be over-stated. If you were told not to think about an orange bus and definitely not an orange bus with blue stripes and pink ears, what is in your mind right now? Even if you have been able to focus on something other than an orange bus with blue stripes and pink ears, you almost certainly had that in mind before you switched to something else. That takes effort.

However, by focusing on what you *do* want, rather than what you *don't* want, your mind is able to do that much more easily.

Let's take a few presentation-specific examples:

	Negatively stated (away from)	Positively stated (towards)
Example 1	I don't want them to be bored	I want them to be inspired
Example 2	I don't want them to delay their decision	I want them to agree immediately
Example 3	I don't want them to be confused	I want them to be clear

If you can imagine yourself thinking about content to avoid boredom, as in example 1, your presentation might come across as frantic and 'trying too hard'. You have probably encountered people at parties who laugh too loudly at jokes, or talk too much. They come across as desperate to be liked but the effect is that they push people away by this need.

By focusing on your audience being inspired rather than bored, you are likely to create a more relaxed yet motivational content and ambience. An inspirational speech needs to engender respect and anyone who appears overly concerned about being entertaining loses credibility. It is the difference between 'doing' and 'being'. 'Doing' comes across as mechanical, unnatural and deliberate whereas 'being' comes across as being authentic, real, natural. By being authentic, you are more likely to be inspirational.

As the singer, Pink, said 'put the same amount of effort into letting go' and you are more likely to be in your flow and, if you are in your flow, you are more likely to be inspirational.

In example 2, the difference is between pushing and drawing-in; pressurizing and attracting. If you are more concerned about avoiding delay, your message is more likely to be pushy and perhaps even intimidating. Can you remember a time when someone was pushy with you? What effect did that have? Did you immediately roll over and ask 'Of course. Where can I sign?' Or did you resist, make excuses and decide that, above all else you wanted to 'think about it'?

Most people have an inbuilt reaction to being pushed and that is to push back. Yet what you want is for them to accept readily. This requires a whole different set of behaviours and a more facilitative approach.

Helping someone to decide immediately requires that you make it a no-brainer for them to say 'yes' – that there is so much in it for them it feels natural to agree with your proposal because they know that you have their best interests at heart. This knowledge enables you to rethink your presentation in a much more constructive way.

Avoiding confusion is a very different thing to creating clarity. If 'avoiding confusion' is your outcome, as in example 3, this is likely to create a presentation that explains in far too much detail and with too many words. This is likely to cause the confusion you are trying to avoid.

If your focus is to create clarity, this opens the mind to a more conducive approach which facilitates the comprehension you seek. It is like putting a key in the lock of your creative mind, releasing ideas that your mind would have been closed to in the 'avoiding' role.

The catch in all of this is that many people think in terms of 'away-froms' which just sends you into a tailspin because it isn't focused on what you want – the 'towards'.

COACHING SESSION 7

'Towards' thinking

If you feel that you get stuck in 'away from' thinking try the following simple process:

1 Identify what it is you want to avoid.

2 Name its opposite(s).

3 Check which of these you actually do want.

So, in example 1 above:

1. Avoid boredom.

2. Opposite of boredom: inspiration, motivation, interest, fascination.

3. Check which of these you actually do want.

In example 2:

1. Avoid delay in decision.

2. Opposite of delay in decision: immediate agreement, sign-up, instant permission, on the spot 'yes'.

3. Check which of these you actually do want.

In example 3:

1. Avoid confusion.
2. Opposite of confusion: clarity, understanding, comprehension.
3. Check which of these you actually do want.

COACHING SESSION 8

Create a positive outcome

Think about an upcoming presentation you have and create a positive outcome for it:

In thinking about the outcome you want to achieve, what style of presentation might best suit that?

Formal ☐

Informal ☐

Talking to ☐

Eliciting feedback ☐

Discussions ☐

Other ☐

THE TITLE

You can have some fun deciding the title of your presentation. This can create a level of anticipation which will engage your audience. Here are some examples:

- **How to** Present with Confidence

- **The Zen of** Presentations

- **Warning:** Presentations Can Improve Your Career

- The **Presentation Secrets** of Steve Jobs

- **The 10 Mistakes** Presenters Make

- How to be a **Presentation Sensation**

- **The Seven Laws of** Presentation Success

If you are implementing a new Customer Relationship Management (CRM) system when people prefer their manual notes, the following might be suitable options:

- Every Ending is a New Beginning – Why Now is the Time for CRM

- Customer Relationship Management – To Lead or to Follow?

- What Our Competitors Want Us to Believe about CRM and Why We Should Ignore Them

COACHING SESSION 9

Choose your presentation heading

Think about your upcoming presentation and brainstorm some headings below.

Of these, which would create the most positive impact and anticipation?

Does the heading promise more than you can deliver or is it set at the right level?

STRUCTURE

A typical structure for a presentation is as follows:

Opening	Content	Closing
10%	80%	10%

As the old adage goes, 'Tell them what you are going to tell them, then tell them, then tell them what you've told them'. One of the reasons for this is that people remember best what you have said at the beginning and the end of your presentation than they do anything in between. So, your opening and closing remarks need to be a) powerful and b) support your content.

COACH'S TIP

Before you start

Before you start working on your structure, you need to know how long you have available to do your presentation. Then you can start working on what should go into it.

OPENING YOUR PRESENTATION

Most presentations start with an introduction – your name and job title. This is OK but not nearly as powerful as a fact, a quotation or something a little controversial that will attract and hold the audience's attention.

There are four purposes to your opening:

1. To engage

2. To introduce yourself

3. To set a framework and expectations with your audience

4. To communicate housekeeping matters, if appropriate.

Let's take them one at a time.

Engage

A fact Think about starting your presentation with a fact to capture their imagination. For example, if you are presenting on the importance of a healthy diet in protecting against cancer, you might start with:

'325,000 people were diagnosed with cancer in 2010. That is enough to fill the O2 arena 16 times over. And it's the number one fear – ahead of debt, loss of job, knife crime, and presenting.'

Develop anticipation Every good novel will create anticipation from one chapter to the next – it's why they call them page-turners. How can you do the same with your presentation? Build anticipation at the beginning, and potentially throughout your presentation. For example:

'I am going to share with you something today which will transform the way that you work. It is unlike anything you have seen before – it's exciting and I can't wait to share it.'

The downside of this technique is that if you build up too much anticipation and deliver a damp squib, you will leave people feeling disappointed, so keep it real.

An image or cartoon In 1921 Frederick R. Barnard said, 'A picture paints a thousand words' and it certainly helps to communicate a concept more easily than words could ever do. The following graphic may work if the team are behind schedule on a project. It can inject a sense of urgency without you having to beat them up.

Do make sure the image (or cartoon) supports your message. Also, make sure that you have rights to use the message. Appendix 1 contains a list of reputable sources for images. Many thousands are available by searching on a particular subject using keywords, just as you would on an internet search engine.

A quotation Quotations are a great way to introduce an idea in a way that is indirectly attached to you so your audience is more open to what you have to say. This uses one of Robert Cialdini's six key principles of influencing: authority. For example, if you are trying to implement a change initiative against much resistance, the following quotation might help:

'Charles Darwin said "It is not the strongest of the species that survives, nor the most intelligent, but the one most responsive to change".'

Your audience may be more willing to accept Darwin and his theory of evolution as an authority figure on the importance of change over your desire to restructure the company. However, do make sure that there is a direct link between your chosen quotation and the point that you want to make. It should expand thinking and stimulate engagement.

Ask a question A question draws attention and raises energy. So, if you are presenting after lunch when people are feeling drowsy, it can be really helpful in drawing people in. For example:

'How many live websites do you think there are worldwide right now?'

If your presentation is to teach people how to optimize their website, this will hook people in right away and their minds will be buzzing. By the way, the number was 366,800,000 in 2011. If you make your presentation about how on earth you are supposed to be found in among that lot, you will have them captivated.

It doesn't work if you just ask 'Is SEO Important?' because that is a closed question which elicits a 'yes' or 'no' response. It does little, if anything, for the energy of the room because there is little work for the mind to do. 'How important is SEO?' is better but not by much. You want to make a real impact and capture their imagination.

Personal introduction

If some members of the audience do not know you, introduce yourself with your name, position and company name, for example:

'Hello, my name is Alex Jordan and I am the Senior Partner at SEO Solutions.'

If you have a strong opening statement, your personal introduction will carry more weight.

Set a framework and expectations

People like to know what to expect and in this section of your opening you should set out the framework for your presentation and expectations with the audience. They will want to know whether they can ask questions during or after your presentation. It should also put your audience at ease, help you to create rapport and give them the benefits of being there. In this way, they are with you from the beginning. You also need to go through the agenda and any ground rules you might have.

Housekeeping

If you are conducting an event to the public or offsite, it may be necessary to include in your opening some 'housekeeping' items. This need only take a minute and should include:

1. Where the fire exits are.

2. What to do in case of fire.

3. Where the toilets are.

4. Break-times and what to do during breaks (i.e. refreshments will be provided in the room / there are plenty of coffee-houses locally / refreshments are provided in the lobby).

An opening section might go something like this:

Engage	'How many live websites do you think there are worldwide right now?'
	Your options here are:
	• Gather about three responses – more than this and it will lose impact. Make it fun and energized.
	• Get them to split up into groups of two to three to discuss their answer – this gets them talking to each other and about the subject, which creates a nice energy in the room. You will then ask each group for their answer and decide who is closest to the real answer.
	• Deliver the answer as part of your introduction. You need to make it clear from your body language that you are not expecting them to respond.
	You might even see how shy or forthcoming your audience is and simply go with the flow as to which method you think will work best with this particular group.
	'The number is 366,800,000 – that's more than the entire population of the United States of America and Canada combined.'
	This is more powerful than saying 'This is more than the population of America and Canada.'
Personal introduction	'Hello, my name is Alex Jordan and I am the Senior Partner at SEO Solutions – the award-winning optimization experts, so you know you are in very safe hands today.'
Set framework and expectations	'I will be talking to you about the secrets of the most successful websites in getting seen by their target market above their competitors.
	I want you to get the very most out of today so do feel free to ask any questions as we go along. We have quite a tight schedule, so if your question is outside the scope of my presentation, I will capture it on my Parked Questions Flipchart and see if we can handle it after my presentation or during the coffee break. Is that OK with you?
	So, the outline for today is to:
	• Explore the nature and importance of search engine optimization in building a profitable business.
	• Discover how to conduct an effective keyword search.
	• Learn effective link-building methods.
	• Find out how to write SEO-friendly blog.
	• Understand how to integrate your SEO with social media.
	By the end of the session you will have the key components of your very own SEO campaign to implement right away.'
	You will notice that each of the bullets starts with a powerful action word which builds expectation and excitement – this is going to be good!

Housekeeping	'Before we begin, there are some housekeeping points to share with you. In the unlikely event of fire, the fire exit is at the back of the room and you should make your way into the car park's assembly point. If you experience that other kind of emergency, the toilets can be found in the corridor on the right-hand side.
	The presentation will run until 12.30 and we will have a break at 10.45 for 20 minutes. Refreshments will be served in the adjoining room.
	Are we ready? OK, let's begin.'

CONTENT

Around 80 per cent of your presentation is the actual content. This is where you get to make your key points in as impactful a way as possible. In doing this, do be wary of giving too much information as this may confuse – you want to give enough to inform but not so much that your message gets foggy.

COACHING SESSION 10

Information

People tend to do three things when they receive information:

Distort

People can twist things to fit their expectations of your meaning. The implication here is that you need to be very clear.

An example of distortion is the image above. What do you see? A vase? Or two people looking at each other?

Think about your message: what distortions might your audience make?

What can you do to guard against this?

Delete

People tend to delete information that they do not see as relevant or that does not fit in with their expectation.

> Paris
>
> in the
>
> the springtime

What do you see written in the box above?

Most people will see Paris in the springtime. It actually says:

Paris in the the springtime.

Because 'the' appears twice, it is ignored. People delete what they don't expect. Again, it is important that you are very clear in your communication. Less is more.

Think about your message: what deletions might your audience make?

What can you do to guard against this?

Generalize

This is where people make universal 'truths' about what is being said, for example using language like 'always', 'never', 'all men are ...', 'all women are ...', 'presentations are ...'. The implication is that you need to be careful to ensure that people are interpreting the information as you intended them to.

Think about your message: what generalizations might your audience make?

What can you do to guard against this?

ANTICIPATING QUESTIONS

Before you begin, decide in advance in what way you would like to include or involve your audience, if at all. Whether you do or not, your audience may have questions during your presentation and it is useful to consider what these might be in advance and how you would like to handle them. You want to spend as much time as possible on this section as you don't want to be blindsided by a show-stopping question that affects your credibility if you don't answer it well.

 COACH'S TIP

Prepare well

The time you invest in this part of your preparation is priceless. Prepare well with strong messaging and anticipating questions that may come up.

Think about all your audience members as you do this. What are their hot buttons? Their concerns? Their hidden agendas? If there are too many people in your audience to do this, take a sample group which should include your main detractor and your biggest fan.

COACHING SESSION 11

Presentation questions

Think about an upcoming presentation you have to make. What are *all* the questions that could possibly come up?

Anticipated question	Answer

Continue on a separate page if necessary.

KEY POINTS

Next, consider what key points you want to make during your presentation. In Alex's example above, these are:

- **Explore** the nature and importance of search engine optimization in building a profitable business.

- **Discover** how to conduct an effective keyword search.
- **Learn** effective link building methods.
- **Find out how** to write SEO-friendly blogs.
- **Understand** how to integrate your SEO with social media.
- For each individual to have the key components of your very own SEO campaign to implement right away.

The highlighted words suggest a teaching element, and you need to think about how you want to achieve this.

Objective	Possible approach
Explore the nature and importance of search engine optimization in building a profitable business	Brainstorm as a group and flipchart answers
Discover how to conduct an effective keyword search	This may involve one or more of the following: • A personal reflection on what key words they believe their clients might use to find them • Working in pairs having them come up with key words for each other's business • A live demonstration on the internet
Learn effective link building methods	This may be a slideshow with screenshots to help illustrate.
Find out how to write SEO-friendly blogs	This could involve a case study. The options are: • Individually • In pairs or small groups • As a group interaction facilitated by you • As a slideshow presentation.

For each individual to have the key components of your very own SEO campaign to implement right away.	This may be by way of a template for individuals to complete and could be demonstrated by you first if it seems complicated.
	
	Depending on time available, it may include sharing. Again, the options are:
	    ■ In pairs
	    ■ Volunteers from the audience sharing
	    ■ Everybody sharing
	
	The benefits of sharing are that it enhances group learning and gives people more ideas. It is energizing and positive. However, it makes it more challenging to manage time.

COACHING SESSION 12

Presentation key points

In thinking about your own upcoming presentation, what are the key points you want to make?

There are other things to consider when making your key points.

Stories

People love stories. Factual or metaphorical, both hold the same power to captivate the imagination of your audience. Steve Jobs was arguably the best corporate storyteller of them all.

In his 2005 Stanford address, he used stories to motivate the graduates to outstanding effect. He chose to tell three stories of his own life.

The first he called 'Connecting the Dots' and this was to help the graduates understand how what happens in your formative years becomes part of making you who you are. His biological mother allowed him to be adopted on condition he went to college. His adoptive parents spent their life savings on this but he *dropped out* as he couldn't see how relevant it was to his future. But in doing so he *dropped into* the classes that did interest him. This is a wonderful use of paradox, which he uses elsewhere in his speech. He followed his intuition and one of the courses he dropped into was calligraphy. This was a foundation for his interest in beautiful graphics and typography. At the time it seemed to have no practical application but he followed his heart and, ten years later, used this skill in the development of the Mac. His message was that you have to trust what your gut tells you and follow your heart. It is only later that you will see how all the dots of your life lead you to who you want to be.

The second story was about 'Love and Loss'. In this he talked about the time he got fired from his own company. He was a public failure, but realized that he still loved what he did so he decided to start all over again. He had been rejected but he was still in love with his work. He talked about the *heaviness* of success being replaced by the *lightness* of being a beginner and it was this lightness that freed him up for his most creative period. He explains that your work is going to fill a large part of your life and the only way to be truly satisfied is to do what you believe is great work and the way to do that is to love what you do. He tells the students 'If you haven't found it yet, keep looking, don't settle.'

His third story was about 'Death' where he explained that the ultimate test of whether you are following your path is to ask yourself 'if today were the last day of my life would I want to do what I am about to do today?' If he noticed that the answer was 'no' too many days in a row, he knew he needed to change something. He explained that when you face death (as he had recently done), all pride and fear of failure falls away. Knowing you are going to die is the best way of avoiding the trap of thinking you have something to lose. There is no reason not to follow your heart. He beautifully explained that death is very likely the single best invention of life. Your time is limited so should not be wasted by living someone else's life or letting other people's opinions drown out your own voice.

Finally, he weaved in the story of a business he had admired, The Whole Earth Catalogue. In their final issue their farewell message, written on the back, was 'Stay hungry, stay foolish.'

He used this as his closing remark, reinforcing all of his previous points. He makes a few errors in his speech which he either corrects or ignores. He reads his speech from beginning to end but reads with passion and authenticity.

His storytelling is humbling, honest and rich with texture so you feel you are in his story with him. It is well worth the 15 minutes of your time to see a master in action: http://www.youtube.com/watch?v=UF8uR6Z6KLc

Illustrating complicated points

Sometimes it can be difficult to appreciate a particular point, so try using a different illustration to create the emphasis you are looking for. For example:

- If you are thinking about the height of something – as high as two double-decker buses one on top of the other.

- If you are talking about the width of something – the width of four football pitches.

- Instead of thinking about the amount of money you want to save on the bottom line, think about the value of this in terms of something positive the audience will appreciate. For example, the number of new staff it will pay for, or the number of jobs it will save.

This creates a picture which helps your audience understand more clearly.

Data is confusing so it is important, as Albert Einstein said, that you should make it as simple as possible, but no simpler. In this regard you should only show the level of data that illustrates your overall message and nothing more. Ask yourself: 'How does this illustrate …?'

Do use colour to highlight the main point, only to the degree that it clarifies your message. Too much contrast, colour and imagery can confuse rather than clarify.

Metaphors

A metaphor is a story, or a figure of speech which has symbolic meaning. For example, the following quotation by Groucho Marx might suit a speech to the NHS about the importance of getting people well quickly so that a new patient can receive treatment: 'A hospital bed is a parked taxi with the meter running'.

To write your own metaphors, you might want to think of your problem in a different way. You can be freestyle or directed. Ask yourself:

1. Freestyle

    i.   This problem/subject is like …

2. Directed

    ii. In what way is this problem/subject like a tree?

    iii. In what way is this problem/subject like a double-decker bus?

For example, in talking about a change initiative you might say:

a. 'This change initiative is like a tree – we have our roots firmly in the ground, we are strong but our branches can flex to our environment – if we weren't able to flex, we would break. It is this flexibility that helps us survive.'

b. 'This change initiative is like a tree, we are going through another season. We need to shed the old leaves so that new leaves can grow and the tree can flourish – change is the natural order of life.'

c. 'This change initiative is like a double-decker bus. We are all going in the same direction. We are all in this together. We are driven by market forces but our conductor guides us through so we navigate our course effectively. We are free to get off if we don't like where we are going, and there are others who may choose to get on the bus with us. But the bus is going to our destination and we would like you to join us on that journey.'

COACH'S TIP

You can really have fun with metaphors. They can bring life and texture to your presentation.

COACHING SESSION 13

Your presentation subject

So, thinking about the subject of your presentation·

How is it like a flashlight?

How is it like a lake?

Finish this sentence. My subject is like … (and then go on to explain how):

CHARTS

Pie charts

Pie charts help you to compare components by percentage proportion of the whole. For example, of all the cakes sold, this pie chart shows very clearly which is the biggest seller for the whole period and how the others compared. Various colour options can be used for pie charts but the variations can be too subtle to distinguish between one item and another so make sure you choose a colour scheme that shows up clearly.

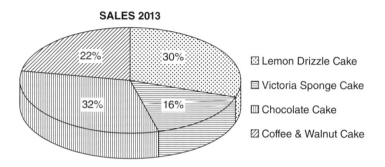

Column charts

Column charts show variations over time, for example, the number of sales of each cake in each quarter to see if there is a theme – is lemon drizzle cake more popular in Q1 or Q2? Which cake sells the most in Q4?

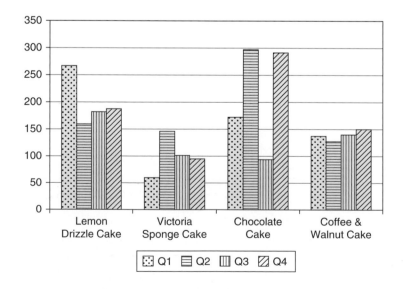

Bar charts

Bar charts show ranked comparisons between items. This example shows how each cake performed in each quarter and overall. So, to demonstrate which cake sold best in the first quarter (the dotted column), look at all the dotted components. This shows that lemon drizzle cake sold more in Q1 but that chocolate cake was the overall best seller for the year.

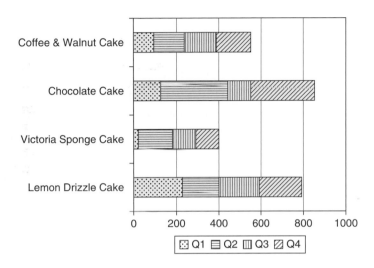

Line charts

Line charts show variation comparison over time. This has similar information to the column chart but it is easier to see the trend as, rather than showing in separate columns for each month, they are shown in a continuous line.

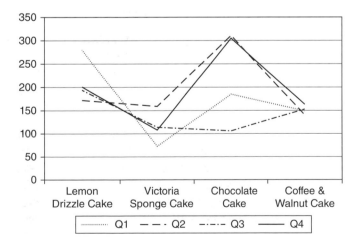

In Chapter 8, we will explore more options in presenting your data.

SUMMARY

Your summary should take about 10 per cent of your entire presentation and summarize what you have covered with your main take away point. When writing this section, think to yourself, 'What is the last thought I want to leave them with?'

The worst thing is to have a strong opening, great content and then to have your ending wither away. 'That's it really' is often used as a close and really undermines everything that precedes it.

A strong close might go something like this: 'So we have looked at the **importance** of Search Engine Optimization in getting your website seen by the right people, we have explored three of the most **powerful** methods, and now you have your own SEO strategy to **implement right away**.

Then, a short soundbite: 'SEO – visitors to your website, sales of your products, profit for your business.'

If appropriate, include a call to action: 'I would like to invite you to offer you a 25 per cent discount off an SEO audit, available to you if booked today. Simply call us on ...'.

You may also want to include the following, if appropriate:

- Next steps
- Q&A
- Contact details.

 COACH'S TIP

How long should your presentation be?

Your presentation should be long enough to get your message across but not so long that people lose interest and disengage.

A WORD ABOUT FLOW

Your presentation should flow naturally from one subject to the next. As you talk, it helps to create smooth transitions with a 'signpost' which brings the audience with you and gives them a chance to ask questions, if you want them to. For example: 'Now that we have talked about the importance of investing in this new system, we will go on to explain the implementation plan. Before we do that, does anyone have any questions so far?'

This will make your presentation sound smooth and natural.

CREATING YOUR PRESENTATION CONCEPT

Now that you have a general idea about what might go into your presentation, it is time to start planning. To begin, gather together some sticky notes, wallpaper and pens. Roll up your sleeves and get comfortable. You will need either a very large table or a good bit of wall space.

COACHING SESSION 14

Creating your presentation concept

Get yourself some sticky notes and a large piece of paper or a whiteboard and consider the following:

1. Determine why you are doing the presentation.

2. Decide on your outcome.

3. Establish your core message

4. Brainstorm all the points you want to make and place each one on a sticky note. Place these on your paper or whiteboard – you need a lot of space for all your ideas. ALL ideas are good at this stage. You absolutely don't want to start editing your ideas out yet because it blocks creativity. If you start judging your ideas here, you will stop the flow from one idea to another which can bear delicious fruit for your presentation. So have fun, take your time in this stage and don't stop until you have nothing left.

5. Determine the pros and cons of each point. Think about:

   i   the degree to which they help you meet your outcome

   ii how they harness the imagination and agreement of your audience members

   iii how they might create problems with your audience.

6. Now is the time to eliminate those ideas that are not conducive to your positive outcome and think about how to address any issues that might arise from your content.

7. Group your sticky notes into themes.

8. Now you are ready to create a structure for your presentation. Remember the note about flow – what is a natural flow for your presentation? Do remember to consider whether and how you want audience participation as this will affect the time needed.

9. Extend your structure to include your opener, the content and the close.

   i   Check in with yourself:

   ii Does this look right?

   iii Does it feel right?

   iv Does it sound right?

   v   Is it logical?

vi Is it easy to understand?

vii Does it fit into the time slot available to you?

x. Do you feel:

xi. Positive?

xii. Worried?

10. If you are not feeling positive, you need to keep at it until it is right.

The beauty of the sticky note method is that it is so easy to move things around as you develop your ideas. It's low-tech but effective.

DEALING WITH CREATIVE BLOCKS

There will be times when you want to communicate something but can't think of the right way to put it. This is called a creative block. The best way to deal with it is to set yourself an outcome and then leave it. Perhaps you could take a walk or make a cup of tea. Or maybe you need to sleep on it. Your mind will work on it and the idea will come to you.

DECIDING ON YOUR METHOD

Now is the time to decide what method you want to use (see Chapter 8), and how you want your audience to interact, which we covered earlier in this chapter.

SOURCES OF RESEARCH

You may need to research your subject and there are many avenues available to help you:

- The internet is the cheapest and most available but you need to be careful because some of the information is not validated
- Books
- Magazines
- Newspapers
- Professional journals
- Other people in the field
- Colleagues
- Interviews
- Focus groups

- Surveys. Survey Monkey (http://www.surveymonkey.com) produces an online survey so that you can gather input and feedback in preparation for your presentation. Examples include:

  - Customer satisfaction surveys
  - Employee satisfaction surveys
  - Marketing surveys
  - Product feedback surveys.

 COACH'S TIP

Surveys

An example of a survey is given in the quiz in Coaching session 1 (Chapter 1): Presentations and You.

COACHING SESSION 15

Preparing for your presentation

If you were to conduct a survey in preparation for your presentation, what questions would you ask?

MEMORY AIDS

One of the biggest nightmares for you as a presenter is to forget what you want to say. There are a few ways to help you remember:

Mind map

Whereas the concept of visually mapping information was used centuries ago, it was popularized by Tony Buzan in the mind map. This is a visual representation of ideas and information. It can be used for brainstorming, so you could use it at the conceptual stage of your presentation as an alternative.

However, it is also a powerful memory aid. To make your own mind map, have your focal theme in the centre of your map. It is helpful to use colours for different elements of your presentation. Each idea is linked and grouped around sub-groups.

Here is an example for you:

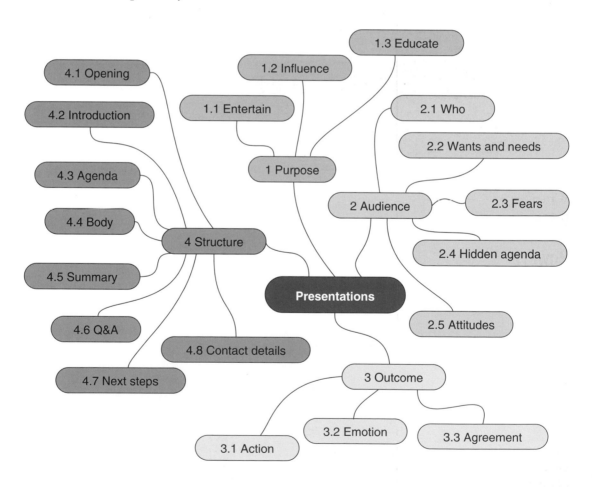

Slides

Your presentation tool – whether it is slideshow or a binder – can be used as a prompt to what you are going to say. However, it cannot contain too much information – there may be things you want to remember to say that are inappropriate to put onto a slide. For example:

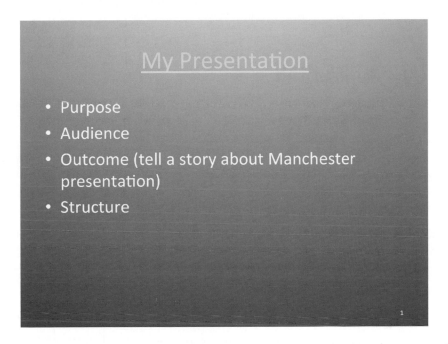

Whereas you may want to remember to tell the story of the Manchester presentation, it would be inappropriate to include it in your visuals.

PowerPoint note pages

PowerPoint allows you to print note pages. This is one slide per page with a space below on which you can include notes. In this way, the audience sees your slides but not the notes you make.

Simply print out a set of note pages for yourself and use these as your prompt.

Note cards

A5 note cards are the traditional memory aid. They are discreet, low-tech and simple. All you need to do is put key points on cards – just have one main point per card with a couple of short bullets points to support it. You can also use your cards as a cue for particular visual aids, such as 'flipchart ideas', or activities, for example 'ask the audience if they have experienced this'. You can also use them to template specific flipchart constructs you want to build.

COACH'S TIP

Note cards

Your note cards need to be printed clearly and put in sequence. For added insurance, do number them. In this way, if you drop your cards, you can quickly put them back in order so that you can proceed with your presentation with confidence.

PRESENTATION TIME PLAN

You can create a presentation time plan and use it to incorporate any specific activities, points or visual aids you want to include in your presentation.

Visual aid	Item	Mins	Timing
Slide 1	Quotation	1	0900–0901
Slide 2	Introduction Tell them about my presentation journey	7	0901–0908
Pre-prepared flipchart	Agenda flipchart Place on wall	5	0908–0913
Pre-prepared flipchart	Ground Rules flipchart Place on wall	2	0913–0915
Slide 3	The Nature and Importance of SEO Group brainstorm on flipchart	10	0915–0925
Slide 4	Effective keyword search	60	0925–1025
PC and projector	Internet demonstration	20	1025–1045
Slide 5	Break	20	1045–1105
Slide 6	Brainstorm keywords in pairs for cake-making business	10	1105–1115
Flipchart	Group feedback	10	1115–1125
Slide 7	Personal reflection time for own business	10	1125–1135

See Appendix 3 for checklist.

ONLINE RESOURCE

Presentation Time Plan

A downloadable version of this template is available for your use from

www.TYCoachbooks.com/Presenting

Even if you are using a slideshow presentation, you may also want to have flipcharts which you can dot around the room to refer to throughout your presentation, as in the case above. These are useful as reminders or signposts. Here are some examples that would be pre-prepared. There may also be flipcharts you develop as you progress through your presentation:

AGENDA

- **Introductions**
- **The Nature and Importance of SEO**
- **Effective Keyword Search**
- **Link Building Methods**
- **SEO Friendly Blogs**
- **Developing your Own**
- **Campaign**
- **Summary**

GROUND RULES

- **Phones off**
- **No hogging, frogging or bogging**
- **Confidentiality**
- **Keep to time**
- **Questions**
- **Park Issues**

We will explain hogging, frogging and bogging in Chapter 12.

ELICITING CONTRIBUTIONS

There may be times when you want to get contributions from your audience. There are various ways you can do this:

Asking You can ask a simple question, such as 'Does anyone have any examples they would like to share?'

Flipchart Ask the entire audience for their ideas and write them down on a flipchart.

Group brainstorming Ask the audience to split up into groups and brainstorm their input which they then write onto flipcharts. You can then either:

- Ask an individual from each team to communicate their input to the entire audience.

- Go round the room eliciting one contribution at a time which you then put onto a single flipchart at the front of the room. This will populate your main chart with everybody's ideas and you don't have any repetition.

GETTING AN IDEA OF THE LEVEL OF AGREEMENT ABOUT A SUBJECT

There will be times when you not only want to get your audience's thoughts, but actually want to know how much that thought is reflective of others in the room. There are a couple of ways to do this:

- Ask people to raise their hands if they agree with a specific point.

- When you flipchart a lot of ideas, give people sticky dots to use to vote on which ideas they agree with the most. This works well when there are lots of flipcharts and has the added advantage of being moderately discreet – it is often easier to vote with dots than it is to say what you really think in front of a large audience.

PARK ISSUES TECHNIQUE

People are bound to ask questions that fall outside the scope of your presentation but, in order to retain rapport, it is important that they feel that you have heard them. The easiest way to do this is to capture those points on a flipchart to be discussed at some other time, either during the break, after the meeting or at another meeting.

HOW NOT TO ALIENATE YOUR AUDIENCE

Last but not least in this chapter about structure and content, your presentation should focus mainly on the audience rather than yourself. A presenter who talks about themselves too much will completely alienate the audience. Compare the following:

- **Example 1 I** am very well qualified to help **you** learn about presenting with confidence. **I** have helped many people. **I** have done lots of presentations **myself**. **I** have also studied the subject in much depth.

- **Example 2 You** are here because **you** want to present with more confidence. During this presentation **I** want to share with **you** tools and techniques which will help **you** to do just that. It will address all **your** concerns and provide **you** with strategies to help **you**.

In Example 1 the ratio is 5:1. In Example 2 the ratio is 1:7.

Which sounds more compelling? Who would you like to listen to more?

Make your presentation more about them than it is about you and you will increase your ability to influence exponentially.

Efforts and courage are not enough without purpose and direction.

John F. Kennedy

 NEXT STEPS

In this chapter you have looked at how to set a clear and positive outcome for your presentation which can then guide all of the content. You have seen the importance of a strong title and some examples of these.

You have learned to structure the content so as to engage your audience in different ways with some examples to guide you. You have seen how people distort, delete and generalize information which has implications for your content. You have also learned about the different types of memory aide you can employ so that everything is covered. Finally, you have started to look at eliciting and managing contributions from the audience.

In the next chapter you will learn about how to use visual aids effectively.

TAKEAWAYS

This is your opportunity to take stock of what you have learned from this chapter. You might want now to choose other chapters and exercises to focus on, or you can continue to work through the whole book if this fits your needs more.

Think about an upcoming presentation that you have.

Brainstorm your ideas

Decide how you would like to structure your presentation.

What would be a strong opener?

What would be a strong close?

Create a presentation time plan using the template in Appendix 3.

8 USING VISUAL AIDS EFFECTIVELY

 OUTCOMES FROM THIS CHAPTER

- In this chapter we will look at the different types of visual aid, the benefits and disadvantages for each and how to use them effectively.

There are many ways of using visual aids to support a presentation. However, they need to be used to enhance your message, not to distract from it, and certainly should not be used to hide behind. Visual aids should complement your words and support your message.

Choices vary from the low-tech (presentation binders, flipcharts) to the high-tech (PowerPoint, slideshows, digital white boards, special effects) and comprise text, images and charts.

In this chapter we will look at the different options, their benefits and disadvantages.

PRESENTATION DISPLAY BINDERS

These hold hard copies of your printed presentation.

Benefits Low-tech, easy to carry around.

Disadvantages Making changes is fiddly.

FLIPCHART

This is a large pad of paper sheets on an easel.

Benefits Easy to use, create as you go, able to attach pages to walls for your audience to view; can be used interactively as they are great for capturing input and brainstorming; can be moved around. Can also complement a slideshow by having pre-prepared slides to show on the walls as you continue your presentation.

Disadvantages Can be illegible if your handwriting isn't clear; difficult to show graphs and tables; errors difficult to correct; difficult to maintain eye contact.

COACH'S TIP

Flipcharts

If your handwriting is poor, use gridded paper and print using the lines to guide you. Write bullet points and headings in a different colour to the text to make it easy to read and interesting.

Examples of generic-style flipcharts might be:

- Ground Rules
- Agenda
- Parked Issues.

For more information on these and how they might be used, visit Chapter 7.

OHPs AND TRANSPARENCIES

OHPs (overhead projectors) and transparencies are practically obsolete but worth a mention, just in case. They use acetates which can be pre-printed or created in situ and projected onto a screen.

Benefits Versatile – can be interactive; give you thinking time between transparencies.

Disadvantages Can get messy if you drop your slides; less slick than PowerPoint.

WHITEBOARD

This is similar to a flipchart, but is fixed and requires special pens.

Benefits Information can be wiped off; errors corrected easily.

Disadvantages Only one board so different 'pages' not visible; static (although sliding boards may be available); difficult to maintain eye contact; if you use the wrong pens, you will not be able to erase your work.

ELECTRONIC WHITEBOARD

The electronic whiteboard links to your computer enabling interaction, combining the function of your screen and the features of a whiteboard. You can use your hand instead of a mouse to operate it. The 'pen tray' allows you to write in different colours as you would on a conventional whiteboard but using your fingers or some other object so you don't have to worry about lost or dried up pens. It is possible to write on the projected image and move things around the board. You can save what you have done and have multiple pages and save them.

Benefits Highly versatile, interactive, multiple pages available, no pens needed.

Disadvantages Expensive, may need some training to use effectively.

LECTERN

Not strictly a visual aid but often available to aid your presentation. These are generally only used in very formal presentations.

Benefits Useful for holding notes and water; can really help you as a prop to feel strong and to hold onto as a means for steadying your hands.

Disadvantages They form a barrier between you and the audience meaning that you need to work doubly hard at making that connection. Short people will need a step to stand on.

POWERPOINT

Microsoft's PowerPoint is the most popular way of conducting presentations. Relatively easy to use and versatile, it can bring a professional touch to your message. In addition, there are many templates you can use as well as SmartArt graphics, a few examples of which are given later in the chapter.

Benefits Very versatile; professional; no papers to carry around (except for back-up); can include video, sound, graphics and charts; many templates available.

Disadvantages Technology can fail; can be too busy and gimmicky.

If you watch Sky News you can see how difficult it is to hear the message of the presenter while watching the ticker tape news flashes – it is sensory overload. In the same way, it is all too easy to overload your audience. This can make all the difference between agreement and opposition, clarity and confusion, action and inaction.

There are many effects you can use, from transitions (how one slide appears after the other) and animations (such as having your slide spin). You can also have sound effects like bombs or cash registers. These bells and whistles are entertaining but tend to distract your audience rather than enhance your message. They are generally a sign of someone not very confident in what they have to say. You want yourself and the slides to speak for themselves.

COACH'S TIP

Slides

Choose background colours that allow text to stand out. Grey on black will be difficult to read. Also, if any members of your audience suffer from colour-blindness, they will not be able to distinguish between red and green. Avoid textured backgrounds as they also make text less clear. Do remember to check what the colour and background look like when your presentation is projected onto the screen you will be using, as this can be different to how it appears on your computer at your desk.

COACH'S TIP

Distance

If you measure your computer screen from the bottom left to the top right in inches, then place a marker the same number of feet away as you had inches (so if your screen measurement is 21 inches, you should place your marker 21 feet away) whatever you cannot see on your slide from that distance is unlikely to be seen at the back of the room.

COACH'S TIP

Blanking the screen

There will be times when you want the audience to listen to you without seeing what is onscreen. This is very easy to do – pressing the B key blanks out your presentation and pressing it again brings it right back when you are ready to put the focus back on your slides.

For a humorous video on how not to use PowerPoint, see the link below. It not only summarizes some of the points brilliantly, but shows you the structure of humour which we explore in Chapter 10: http://www.youtube.com/watch?v=KbSPPFYxx3o

COACH'S TIP

Eye contact

Eye contact with your audience is very important no matter what kind of presentation you choose. If you need to glance at your presentation, do so, but direct your words to the audience.

HOW TO DISPLAY YOUR DATA

There are many options on how to display your information. The following are five separate ways of showing the same kind of information.

Option 1 Bullet points

In this slide, everything is displayed in a simple format. All the words you need are written so you can't forget them, but it is practically useless to your audience who will be faced with the choice of listening to you or reading the slides.

Why Companies Conduct Webinars

- Webinars help you to **generate leads** that you can then convert into sales
- They are an excellent way of **building loyalty** with your existing customer base because you will be giving greater value
- Websites improve your search engine optimization so that you **drive website visits**
- If you conduct the webinar effectively, you can encourage people to go to your website to buy your products which will **drive offline business**
- As you improve your SEO with webinars, more people will become aware of you and that will **increase brand awareness**
- Because people will sign into your webinar, you will be able to **build an in-house database** which can further increase your sales

---

Option 2 Bullet points with reduced content

This is much easier for your audience to read and means that people will be listening to you rather than reading your slides, or reading your slides along with you. It looks less like a manuscript and more like a slide. You are no longer redundant! However, it still doesn't engage the imagination and so is better suited to a logical audience.

Why Companies Conduct Webinars

- Generate leads
- Build loyalty
- Drive website visits
- Drive offline business
- Increase brand awareness
- Build in-house database

Option 3 Pie charts

Pie charts organize the information visually and require that you talk about the different pieces of the pie. Do be careful with the use of colour as some of the offered colour choices make it difficult to differentiate between one piece of the pie and the next.

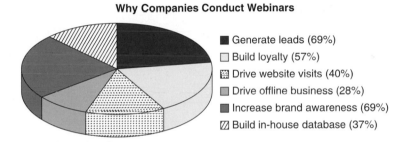

Why Companies Conduct Webinars

- ■ Generate leads (69%)
- □ Build loyalty (57%)
- ▦ Drive website visits (40%)
- ▩ Drive offline business (28%)
- ■ Increase brand awareness (69%)
- ▨ Build in-house database (37%)

Option 4 Images to indicate different parts of your presentation

You can display the same information using imagery; this appeals to the imagination and is more friendly to the creative mind. However, it is a lot of information on one page and may be difficult to take in. You will probably need to point at each image as you talk about it.

Option 5 Images to illustrate different points on a point-by-point build

This has the benefits of option 4 – visuals that appeal to the creative mind and help retention – however it differs in that each slide allows you to introduce one new element at a time. This makes it easier for your audience to take it in and absorb the information more effectively. You will notice that there are three different effects used for each image which adds a subtle dimension to your slides. This is easily done in PowerPoint, by clicking on the image and selecting picture tools.

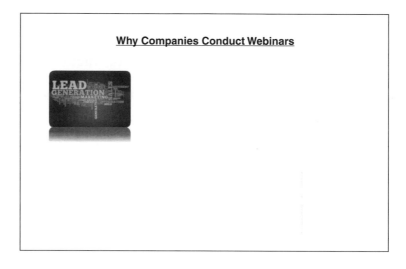

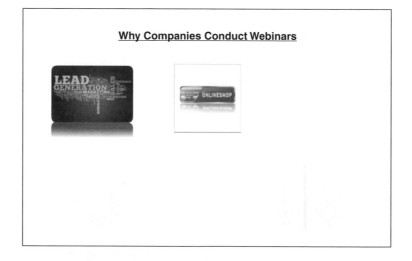

Why Companies Conduct Webinars

Why Companies Conduct Webinars

Why Companies Conduct Webinars

Slides are a matter of personal choice. It is also a matter of thinking about your audience and what they need. Have fun!

SmartArt

In addition, PowerPoint has produced a series of editable and formatted diagrams to help you illustrate complicated points with greater ease. There are many and here are a few examples to show you the type and use of each one. Do check out PowerPoint for more options.

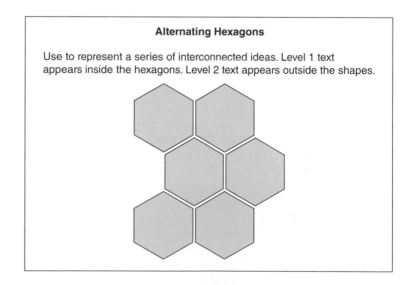

Architectural Layout

Use to show hierarchical relationships that build from the bottom up. This layout works well for showing architectural components or objects that build on other objects.

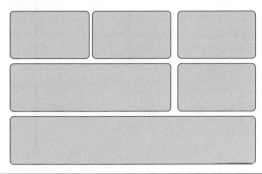

Balance

Use to compare or show the relationship between two ideas. Each of the first two lines of Level 1 text corresponds to text at the top of one side of the centre point. Emphasizes Level 2 text, which is limited to four shapes on each side of the center point. The balance tips towards the side with the most shapes containing Level 2 text. Unused text does not appear, but remains available if you switch layouts.

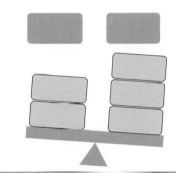

The Basic Block List

Use to show non-sequential or grouped blocks of information. Maximizes both horizontal and vertical display space for shapes.

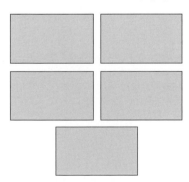

Basic Cycle

Use to represent a continuing sequence of stages, tasks, or events in a circular flow. Emphasizes the stages or steps rather than the connecting arrows or flow. Works best with Level 1 text only.

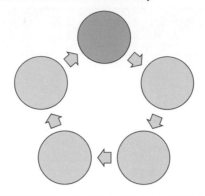

Continuous Picture List

Use to show groups of interconnected information. The circular shapes are designed to contain pictures.

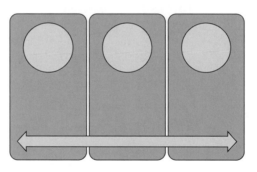

Cycle Matrix

Use to show the relationship to a central idea in a cyclical progression. Each of the first four lines of Level 1 text corresponds to a wedge or pie shape, and Level 2 text appears in a rectangular shape to the side of the wedge or pie shape. Unused text does not appear, but remains available if you switch layouts.

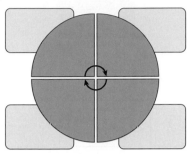

Horizontal Bullet List

Use to show non-sequential or grouped lists of information. Works well with large amounts of text. All text has the same level of emphasis, and direction is not implied.

Non-Directional Cycle

Use to represent a continuing sequence of stages, tasks, or events in a circular flow. Each shape has the same level of importance. Works well when direction does not need to be indicated.

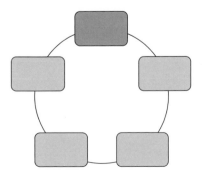

Organizational Chart

Use to show hierarchical information or reporting relationships in an organization. The assistant shape and the Org Chart hanging layouts are available with this layout.

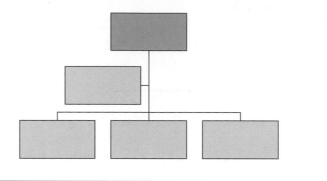

Process Arrows

Use to show information illustrating a process or workflow. Level 1 text appears in the circular shapes and Level 2 text appears in the arrow shapes. Works best for minimal text and to emphasize movement or direction.

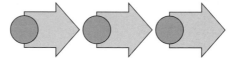

Segmented Pyramid

Use to show containment, proportional, or interconnected relationships.
The first nine lines of Level 1 text appear in the triangular shapes.
Unused text does not appear, but remains available if you switch layouts.
Works best with Level 1 text only.

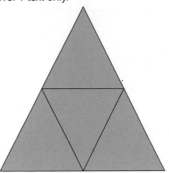

Target List

Use to show interrelated or overlapping information. Each of the first seven
lines of Level 1 text appears in the rectangular shape. Unused text does not
appear, but remains available if you switch layouts. Works well with both
Level 1 and Level 2 text.

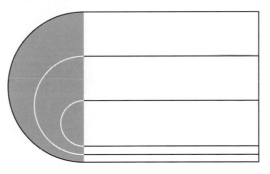

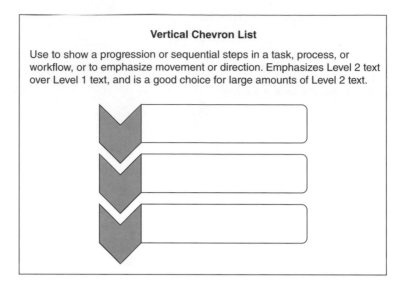

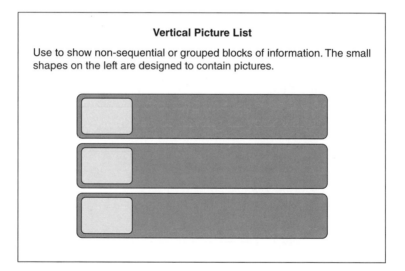

Structure of your slides

Slides will usually follow this structure:

- Header
- Logo (usually in the header or in the footer)
- Presentation title or slide title
- Core of slide – text, image, data
- Footer.

You may want to number your slides as it makes it easy to refer people to the slide if they lose their place in their notes.

There are numerous slide layouts to choose from including:

- Title slide
- Title and content
- Section header
- Two content
- Comparison
- Title only
- Blank
- Content with caption
- Picture with caption.

PREZI

Prezi is a software package which enables you to show your presentation with a zoom facility so that you can focus on specific elements of your presentation – zoom out to get the big picture, or zoom in to drill into the detail. You can also insert images within images and show your entire presentation as one canvas if you wish.

Benefits Easy to use, creative.

Disadvantages Dizzying to watch; takes more time than just a conventional slideshow presentation to put together.

FONTS

The font you select will say something about you and will also make a difference to how much easier it is for someone to read and absorb your message. There are thousands of fonts and they all communicate a subtle message. For example:

Times New Roman	Tahoma
Arial	Comic Sans
Century Gothic	Georgia

TIPS ON USING VISUAL AIDS

- Do keep it professional.

    - Brand your presentation if possible.

    - Make sure each page has a similar look and feel.

    - Use the same font size configuration throughout and make sure it's legible.

    - Use the same typeface throughout.

- Remember to speak to the audience, not your presentation – you want to maintain good eye contact throughout.

- Avoid reading out your slides – if you do, make sure your eye contact is excellent (i.e. always direct your words towards your audience).

- Do not stand between your visuals and the audience.

- When choosing the colour of your slides, think about what different colours convey, i.e. red for passion or anger, blue for calm.

- Do not have more than four colours per slide.

- Demonstrate complicated points visually.

- Images are great – a picture paints a thousand words.

- Graphs should be simple and legible.

- Don't put spreadsheets onto PowerPoint – people can't cope with more than five rows by five columns of data.

- Have one main idea per slide.

- Have just a few words per line as a busy slide is difficult to read.

- Make sure there is lots of white space.

- Aim for font size 24–28 so that it looks like a slide rather than a document.

- Avoid too many slides.

- Check for spelling and grammar (no text speak).

- Use a pointer if necessary (high-tech and low-tech versions available).

> *If your words or images are not on point, making them dance in colour won't make them relevant.*
>
> Edward Tufte

NEXT STEPS

In this chapter you have explored the various types of visual aid which can enhance your presentation from the low-tech presentation display binder to the high-tech electronic whiteboard. You have learned about the pros and cons of each of these so that you can make an informed choice when deciding which to use to best support your message as well as some tips on how to use them effectively. You have seen the various options available for displaying your data and how to structure your slides, should you be using them.

In the next chapter you will learn about how to deal with presentation nerves so that you come across in the most positive light.

👍 TAKEAWAYS

This is your opportunity to take stock of what you have learned from this chapter. You might want now to choose other chapters and exercises to focus on, or you can continue to work through the whole book if this fits your needs more.

Think about an upcoming presentation you have. What visual aids will best serve you?

Think about some data that you need to share. Which method would help you do that so that it's clear for your audience?

Go back over the Coach's tips given in this chapter. Which three will make the biggest difference to your presentation?

9 DEALING WITH PRESENTATION NERVES

 OUTCOMES FOR THIS CHAPTER

- In this chapter we will consider why nerves are good for you, the effect of your beliefs on your confidence and how to develop a positive presentation mindset.

Most people who dread presentations have simply not yet developed the right mindset. However, as our survey revealed, being able to present is critical to your career and your business. If you are confident in yourself, your audience will be confident in you and your influencing skills will be significantly enhanced as a result.

DO I HAVE TO?

The very idea of doing a presentation can send a chill through many people. It can even send a frisson of anxiety and anticipation through the most seasoned speaker who can speed through a myriad of emotions from excitement: 'Fantastic – a great opportunity', to doubt: 'I don't know these people, what if they don't like what I have to say?', or even boredom: 'Not again.'

Glossophobia is the fear of public speaking (or of speaking in general) which comes from the Greek word *glõssa,* meaning 'tongue', and *phobos,* meaning 'fear'.

Now, you may not be suffering from a phobia, but it could be that there is a degree of trepidation which is affecting your confidence whenever you need to present – or even at the suggestion that you might be required to present at some point in the future. In fact, it is estimated that only 25 per cent of people are not affected at all.

Fear can be described as False Evidence Appearing Real and it arises when you are focusing on the negative, such as what people might think of you, or the thought of making a mistake. Thoughts are not real either and our feelings, such as anxiety, are a direct result of our thoughts. So, if you change your thinking, you change how you feel.

WHY NERVES ARE GOOD FOR YOU

You actually need a few nerves to be a success in presenting. The worst kind of presentation is when the speaker is so laid back that they fail to engage the audience, when they can come across as uninterested, or even arrogant.

The best kind of presentation, by contrast, is where the speaker is calm *and* energized, structured *and* flowing, informative *and* engaging.

When you think about presenting, which type do you most associate with?

	Type	Self-Talk	Confidence	Enthusiasm	Engaging
1	Able but bored	I can do this with my eyes shut	High	Low	Low-Good
2	Excited and raring to go	Great – where's the stage	High	High	High
3	Open and willing	I'll be fine	Good	High	Good
4	Nervous but willing	This'll be interesting	Good	Good	Good
5	Nervous but dutiful	Oh no! Do I really have to?	Low	Low	Low-Good
6	Scared and seeking a way out	Get me out of here!	Low	Low	Low

You will see that each type varies according to the level of confidence and enthusiasm and so will impact the likely engagement of your audience. Someone who is too confident is just as likely to be a turn-off as the person who wants to find the nearest exit. If people see you are willing if a little nervous, they are more likely to be on your side.

▢▢ COACHING SESSION 16

How do you know you are nervous?

Nerves can affect people in different ways and symptoms can include one or more of those listed in the table below. Go through the list and, in the middle column, score yourself on a scale of 0–10 as to how that particular symptom is true for you when you think about, or when you are doing, a presentation, where 10 is completely true, and 0 is not true at all.

Increased heart rate		
Perspiration		
Shortness of breath		
Trembling hands		

Dry mouth		
Tension in neck upper back		
Tension in voice		
Quivering voice		
Stuttering		
Going blank		
Blushing		
An urgent need for the loo		
Nausea		
Unable to make eye contact		

Now, think about a time when you were excited as a child. Perhaps on Christmas morning or when you went on a roller coaster. Using the same list, go through and in the right-hand column mark out of 10 the degree to which you experienced each symptom.

It's interesting to note that there is often a remarkable similarity between anxiety and excitement. Was this true for you? What does this tell you about your feelings about presenting?

It is even more interesting to note that excitement can help your presentation success so these feelings can actually work *for* you. And can help your enjoyment too!

THE FIGHT/FLIGHT/FREEZE RESPONSE

When your anxiety levels are high, your body has what is called 'an emotional hijack'. This is characterized by a flood of adrenaline which then causes your body to go into fight, flight or freeze mode at the perceived threat. This is why you get palpitations, you start to sweat (your body trying to cool you down), and you can suffer from tummy upsets or have an urgent need to visit the toilet.

This is a legacy from the days when we were required to fight sabre-tooth tigers and it was really important that we were able to run for our lives so that we weren't eaten for breakfast. Presenting to a group of people doesn't pose that kind of danger (no matter how badly you feel about it) but our brains can't distinguish between what is real and what is imagined. When this emotional part of your brain is triggered, it simply wants to fight its way out of a situation, run from it or freeze in an effort to be invisible.

The great news is that this response is natural and that it passes. Fear is just a feeling: False Evidence Appearing Real. Sometimes, simply acknowledging that feeling is enough to let it pass. It can be the resistance to it that gives it strength.

VISUALIZING SUCCESS

Something that top athletes do is visualize their success prior to an important game or event. When a lot of nervous presenters imagine themselves doing a presentation, they see themselves shaking, beads of perspiration on their brow, head bowed and eyes shifty. They imagine their voice shaking and feel their stomach churning. They will probably imagine all kinds of things going wrong too – the PowerPoint presentation failing, a member of the audience being difficult, themselves stuttering as they try to find the right words. It is no wonder that this 'dress rehearsal' creates a negative template for presentation success.

The movies you play in your mind are very powerful and can manifest as your reality – your mind believes what you feed it.

COACHING SESSION 17

Visualization

If you want to be a confident presenter, try this visualization incorporating the main senses:

- **See** yourself standing confidently, shoulders relaxed, standing tall, arms comfortably by your side, eyes bright and making contact with the audience, an engaging smile on your face and using the stage and/or your visual aids like a true natural. See the audience smiling and showing an interest in what you are saying.

- **Hear** your voice powerful, strong and well modulated and the sound of applause as the audience appreciates an important point you have made.

- **Feel** relaxed and alert in your body, calm in your stomach, and flow in your gestures.

When you imagine this, how does it make you feel about your presentation? Make sure your mental rehearsals are positive and empowering and you will notice your confidence is stronger.

In Chapter 12, we will explore what to do when things go wrong and how to deal with them with grace and ease.

LIMITING BELIEFS

Beliefs are the thoughts that you hold to be true. They are a generalization you make about yourself, or about people, or about the world. They are views held that cannot easily be changed by information or reasoning and are built up through life experiences, upbringing and personality. Beliefs can be empowering – working for you, or limiting – working against you.

They have a powerful, self-fulfilling effect and can really impact your confidence, your behaviour and your experience.

COACHING SESSION 18

Limiting beliefs

Following are some sample limiting beliefs people may have about presenting, together with sample challenges and a corresponding opposing belief. Try the empowering beliefs on for size and see what difference they make to how you feel about presenting:

Sample limiting beliefs	Sample challenges	Sample empowering belief
I'm just not a natural presenter.	Presentation skills can be learned. I couldn't walk until I learned to do that, so I can learn to present too.	I enjoy learning to present naturally.
I am too shy to present.	Shy people can present too. Not everybody has to be an extravert or a comedian.	I can be my natural self and present well.
I have to know everything about my subject before I can present on it.	I know more than most on my subject and, if I'm asked a difficult question, I can get back to them when I have found the answer.	I know more than enough to do a great presentation on this subject.
It's really bad to blush in front of others.	Even if I blush, I can carry on presenting. My message will still be the same and any blushing will fade.	I can present well with our without blushing.

What did you notice about the sample limiting beliefs? How did you feel when you tried them on for size? Did they make you feel more confident or less confident? Did you experience more dread or less dread? Did you feel more empowered or less empowered?

You would not be alone if they made you feel less confident, more dread and less empowered.

Now, how did you get on with the sample empowering statements when you tried those on for size?

The great thing about beliefs is that they can be transformed. Unfortunately, it isn't just a switch that you turn on. However, with practice and repetition, you can begin to think like a confident presenter. It's like building a muscle – you just need to keep working it so that it becomes stronger. You want your new beliefs to be so strong that they become your new default pattern.

COACHING SESSION 19

Identifying your limiting beliefs

List your own negative beliefs below. Do take your time to think about these. They can be hidden away in the corners of your mind. So, get yourself a coffee, sit down and get to work. If you don't find that any come to mind, ask yourself the following question: If I did have a negative belief about presenting, what would it be?

Then just allow your mind to provide the answer – give yourself a bit of space for the answer to come. This is not something to be forced or rushed, but *allowed*.

Now try the following. If (trusted friend/boss/colleague/relative) were to say I had a limiting belief about presenting, what would it be? Complete the following sentences

Presentations are

I am a _____ presenter

COACHING SESSION 20

Limiting beliefs 2

When you have written down your first belief, ask yourself 'what else?' Keep repeating 'what else?' until you really have no more left.

You may find that some of them come to you during the night when your unconscious mind has had a chance to mull it over, so add those in too. The more you flush out, the more you can overcome.

My negative beliefs about presenting

CREATING EMPOWERING BELIEFS

Now that you have identified all of the negative beliefs you have about presenting, think about an empowering alternative belief that you can start practising. These will tend to be the opposite of your negative beliefs. You don't have to believe them just yet – in fact you won't. What you will need to do is affirm them on a very regular basis. This can be particularly powerful when you affirm them in front of a mirror. This is not something you do once or twice. As mentioned, it is a little like developing a muscle and so repetition is going to be very important. The more you repeat the empowering beliefs, the stronger they will become.

COACHING SESSION 21

Developing empowering beliefs

Now that you have flushed out your negative beliefs, think of some positive ones which would counteract them, as in the example in Coaching session 18.

Empowering positive beliefs to develop:

ONE CONVERSATION AT ONCE

One reason why people struggle over their words is because they are having a conversation in their minds about whether they can do something or not (see limiting beliefs above), or they may have worried thoughts about whether they will remember an important point, what the audience thinks about them or what they will do if they make a mistake. A simple strategy to overcome this inner talk is to 'empty your mind' before the presentation, which gives your unconscious mind space to flow. This, of course, presupposes that you have planned and rehearsed your presentation well and that you know your subject. Instead of focusing on the conversation you are having with yourself, focus your attention on being with the audience – what you are doing to help them – and your words will flow much more easily.

WHAT IF?

If you are the kind of person who is constantly worrying about what might go wrong, this will create barriers to your flow. The key is to prepare for all contingencies (see Chapter 12). That's all you need to do and, of course, develop a sense of humour about things going wrong. Mostly what you worry will happen won't. And, if it does, so what? It isn't terminal. All the best presenters make errors but it doesn't stop them from being great. It is all about how they handle it. Mistakes can be:

- ignored
- corrected
- laughed at.

Laughter is a great medicine and, if you learn to laugh at yourself, your audience will laugh with you. If you look embarrassed, they will either sympathize or pity you. Either way, it doesn't really do your credibility much good so it is more beneficial not to take yourself so seriously.

It's also useful to put your worries in context. How likely is it that you will fall over, out of a 100? It is doubtful that it is even 1 out of 100, though your anxiety is in danger of kidding you into believing that it is a foregone conclusion.

So, how likely is it that you will fall on your face?

How likely is it that you will stay standing throughout?

♊ COACHING SESSION 22

Prepare for contingencies

What are you most worried might happen in your presentation?

On a scale of 1–100, how likely is that to happen?

If it did happen, would it be terminal?

If not, what would you plan to do about the problem should it occur?

CONFIDENT BODY LANGUAGE

Confident people show it in their body language before anyone hears their presentation. To show confidence – and to feel it – your body needs to feel relaxed and strong and you need to walk purposefully.

COACH'S TIP

Show confidence

Stand tall and imagine that you have a string pulling up your head so that it sits on top of your neck – your neck should be long.

Body language nerves are displayed by fiddling: with your pockets, your hair, your ears, nose, rings and jangling the change in your pockets. So, keep your hands calm and relaxed with your arms relaxed and by your side. However, you can use your hands and arms to make confident gestures (no, not that kind – no matter how troublesome the audience). Using your hands and arms well can provide animation to your presentation.

Other clues you are nervous are crossing one leg over the other when standing, or standing on the sides of your feet, or having all your weight on one leg. It is much better to have your feet firmly on the ground, evenly spaced. This will make you feel grounded and strong.

BREATHING

How you breathe can have a direct effect on your nerves. To feel calm, you need to breathe deeply. Do some deep breathing before your presentation and notice how it calms you. During your presentation, make sure you are breathing properly, deep into your chest. Not only will you feel more calm and grounded, but your voice will be stronger too.

FIND A SMILING FACE

It can help to find a smiling face in the audience and use it as a positive anchor. An anchor is something that triggers a specific response. So, a smiling face might trigger a feeling of warmth and friendliness from you. This will texture your presentation with warmth and friendliness. However, it is important not to fixate on that one smiling face but to keep coming back to it as you make eye contact with the entire audience. In this way you infuse the whole audience with your warmth and friendliness rather than alienate them as you would if you simply fixated on one person. If there isn't a smiling face (unlikely), think of something or someone who makes you feel warm and friendly – it may be your child, your dog or your spouse.

REFRAME HOSTILITY

What if the audience looks positively hostile? First of all, it's important to remember that this does not necessarily reflect how they feel. Some people look stern when they are relaxed or concentrating, or they may have had a bad experience on their way into the office. It is easy to assume that the perceived hostility is personal. Whereas it may be, it is unlikely to be. Instead, remember the benefits of your presentation, either to the audience, or for a greater purpose.

It can also help to imagine individuals in the audience being vulnerable. We all have times when we feel small – they are no exception. In fact, as a general rule, the more aggressive or hostile an individual, the more they are trying to cover up their own insecurities. There will have been times when they were told off by an authority figure, or when they did something embarrassing. Remembering that puts things into perspective.

 COACH'S TIP

Be strong

We tend to compare our outtakes of life with everyone else's edited highlights, assuming we are somehow less than them. We are not. You are not.

TAKE THE FOCUS OFF YOU

Nervous people tend to focus far too much on themselves – 'Am I blushing?', 'Am I coming across OK?' The great news is that most people don't look as nervous as they feel, so simply ignoring that troublesome inner critic can really help. But, most importantly, focus on your audience instead – 'What do they need from me?', 'How can I help them?', 'Do they need more interaction?', 'Do they need more clarification?' This change of perspective moves you from the nervous novice to the audience-responsive professional.

BE CLEAR OF YOUR PURPOSE AND OUTCOME

When your outcome is clear, all your energies focus on it which increases your level of confidence. Remind yourself why you are doing this, who it will benefit and how.

A STRONG START

There is nothing like a strong start to make you feel good. So, once you have done your deep breathing and assumed your confident posture, begin speaking with a strength of purpose. This is done when you are clear about your outcome (see above) and also when you have memorized your introduction. Practise, practise and practise some more. And, when you have finished, practise it again. It needs to flow, to roll off the tongue. Once you are in your flow, it is easy for everything else to follow through. It is as though your mind has cleared a pathway for your words to be delivered with grace and ease. It's a great feeling!

HYDRATION

Did you know that being dehydrated can affect how you feel? So, the day before and throughout the day of your presentation, do make sure you are drinking plenty of water. Don't wait until you are thirsty to drink a pint of water – sips throughout the day are what your body needs. Not only will you feel calmer but your mind will be clearer too. Dehydration contributes to confused and sluggish thinking, so you have an extra reason to drink plenty of water throughout the day.

 COACH'S TIP

Keep hydrated

Avoid iced water, which can jar the body – water at room temperature is easier on your body and on your nerves.

Aim for six to eight glasses of water a day – more if you drink lots of tea or coffee. In fact, avoid coffee since that can make you feel agitated. Chamomile tea is calming, as is hot water with a good squeeze of lemon.

FEED YOURSELF CALM

Did you know that some foods can make your anxiety worse? Anxiety can be caused by blood sugar problems so anything that increases your blood sugar could be bad for your presentation, for example sugary foods such as biscuits and foods that convert to sugar too quickly, such as white bread.

Foods rich in magnesium and the B vitamins can help your nerves. Magnesium-rich foods include:

Almonds	Apples *	Aubergines
Blackberries	Brazil nuts	Broccoli **
Cabbage **	Carrots *	Cashews
Celery	Cheddar cheese **	Chicken * **
Crab	Dried apricots	Dried dates
Dried figs	Dried prunes	Eggs **
Garlic	Grapes	Green beans
Green leafy veg **	Lettuce *	Milk *
Mushrooms ***	Oats	Onions
Parsley	Peanuts	Pyeas
Potatoes with skins	Raisins	Sweetcorn
Tomatoes **		

* Also high in chromium which is good for blood sugar

**Also good sources of B vitamins which are great for nerves

So, some great calming meals could be:

- Chicken with green leafy vegetables, carrots and jacket potatoes
- Porridge made with milk, dried dates and chopped almonds
- Mushroom, onion and cheese omelette with parsley and tomatoes.

Do remember that healthful eating requires a broad range of foods so do consult a nutritionist for a more personalized recommendation to suit your specific health needs.

EMOTIONAL FREEDOM TECHNIQUE

Emotional freedom technique (EFT) is an energy therapy that can help you to deal with nerves and create a resourceful, confident state. It is easy to use and, with practice, can give you fast results. For a demonstration see http://log.self-help-resources.co.uk/eft-demonstration-by-tricia-woolfrey. (See Appendices for checklists and downloadable resources.) Sample declaration phrases are given below but it is essential that you use a phrase that matches how you are feeling in the moment:

- I feel really nervous about doing this presentation.
- I am worried in case I am asked a question I don't know the answer to.
- I'm terrified that Bob will try to sabotage my presentation.

You can also finish off with a positive phrase, for example:

- I choose to feel calm and confident.

MORE CONFIDENCE TIPS

Sorry, but a little alcohol to loosen you up is *not* a good idea. You can always tell. You become a little too relaxed, a little too lackadaisical and are in danger of playing a little fast and loose with the humour and the stage. The combination of a microphone and a few drinks might seem appealing but can damage your reputation and leave you with regrets. Here are some more tips to help your confidence:

- Make sure you get a great night's sleep the night before (if you have trouble sleeping try the MP3 Sleep Well – see Appendix 1 for further information).

- Focus on how much you care about the audience – this takes your thoughts away from yourself.

- Don't take yourself too seriously.

- Manage negative thinking (read *Think Positive, Feel Good* – see Appendix 1 for further information).

- Join a speaking group.

- Write a presentation on something you really love and practise that first.

- Expand your comfort zone – we learn outside of it, we become stronger outside of it. The purpose is to expand your comfort zone so that you are comfortable with more and more stuff.

- If you aren't already doing so, start using social media. This is a way of you being public with your thoughts in a safer way. When you get used to this you can take it to the next level.

- Be less concerned about what people think about you.

- Turn down the volume on your negative voice and speed it up so that it sounds like Mickey Mouse – it's hard to hear or to take seriously then.

- Stop awfulizing. What you dread is unlikely to happen.

- Remember that most people's nerve symptoms are not visible, or not very visible. And, even if they are, so what?

- Ask questions to get input – engaging your audience can make you feel less 'on show' and more 'part of'.

- Dress for success – if you know you look good, you will feel good too (more in the next chapter).

- If you sweat when you are nervous, wear something that doesn't show it and is lightweight so you feel cooler. Have a freshly laundered handkerchief to mop your brow if necessary.

- If you are shaking, stand with your feet firmly and evenly planted on the ground. If you have a lectern, rest your hands on that. Avoid holding notes as this will make any shaking visible.

- If you have a dry mouth, sip water and gently bite your tongue to produce saliva. Alternatively, you can imagine cutting into a nice, juicy lemon.

- Remember that everybody gets better with practice. Everybody starts somewhere and learning can be part of the fun.

- Last but not least, do read the next chapter which also contains some great tips to give you presentation confidence.

(See Appendices for checklists and downloadable resources.)

> *Courage is resistance to fear, mastery of fear, not absence of fear.*
>
> Mark Twain

NEXT STEPS

In this chapter you have explored the various symptoms of nerves and why some nerves are actually good for your presentation. You have learned various techniques for managing your nerves including visualization, exploring and challenging your limiting beliefs, the effect of your inner-talk and numerous techniques to give you more confidence while you present, including the importance of body language. You have also seen how the effect of a clear purpose and outcome as well as a strong start can boost your confidence.

In the next chapter, you will learn in more depth those techniques which will help you to engage and influence your audience successfully.

👍 TAKEAWAYS

This is your opportunity to take stock of what you have learned from this chapter. You might want now to choose other chapters and exercises to focus on, or you can continue to work through the whole book if this fits your needs more.

What limiting beliefs do you have about presenting?

What challenges do you have for these beliefs?

What empowering belief will better serve you?

Of the confidence tips, which three will make the most difference in developing a magic mindset for you?

10 BUILDING RAPPORT AND CREDIBILITY

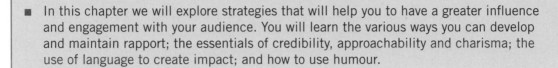

✔ OUTCOMES FROM THIS CHAPTER

- In this chapter we will explore strategies that will help you to have a greater influence and engagement with your audience. You will learn the various ways you can develop and maintain rapport; the essentials of credibility, approachability and charisma; the use of language to create impact; and how to use humour.

Once you have your core message decided, your content and your structure planned, the next important element of successful presenting is being able to engage and influence your audience. They need to feel you are talking to them personally. You need to show a blend of empathy, authority, knowledge and respect.

RAPPORT

Rapport can be considered as a sense of connection, understanding and harmony with your audience. When there is rapport there is trust. When there is trust people will accept your message more readily. It is the foundation of influence and, in a presentation situation, is achieved by various means (all explained in detail as we progress through the chapter):

- Confidence – if you are confident in yourself, people will be confident in you (see Coach's tip)
- Your authenticity – without it there can be no trust
- Matching language
- Positive eye contact
- Honouring values
- Pacing and leading.

In Chapter 4 we explored the difference between confidence and arrogance and these are important considerations when building rapport.

COACH'S TIP

Confidence versus arrogance

Confidence is self-belief with a dash of humility. Arrogance is confidence with a good dose of self-importance and a sense of superiority. Confidence wins the day in positively influencing people in the short- and the long-term. Arrogance may get you short-term buy-in but it makes you vulnerable over time to sabotage and is essentially a rapport-breaker.

To establish rapport you will need to use open gestures, share common ground, understand others' point of view, show respect for their opinion and suspend judgement. Always look for a win–win. It is also important to be aware of cultural differences – business culture but also country culture if appropriate.

AUTHENTICITY

To be authentic is a state of being rather than doing. You cannot 'do' authenticity. In some of the videos that are recommended for your viewing (see 'Consolidating what you have learned, at the end of the book) there are two individuals who shine in their authenticity: Jamie Oliver and Susan Cain. They are very different in their personality and style. But they both come across as very real, unconcerned about whether you like them or not, yet very caring in their approach.

Authenticity comes from a strong sense of self, of your own values and a belief in your message. People have a fairly strong radar for fakery. It is rare for an authentic individual to demonstrate arrogance or self-importance as this will usually stem from someone with something to prove rather than someone who is comfortable in their own skin. Authenticity is also about your words, body language and tone all complementing each other. Giggling when talking about a serious subject will undermine your message. Saying that everyone is happy about the proposition in a flat voice will equally weaken your overall message.

Do not play the comparison game – if you compare yourself to someone else, comparing your worst traits against their best, this will inhibit you from being able to be yourself. Let your true self shine through. You have plenty of positive traits to counterbalance anything you aren't happy with.

Authentic people have more charisma. Charismatic people have a natural rapport, charm and appeal. In her book, *21 Ways and 21 Days to the Life you Want*, Tricia Woolfrey explains that charismatic people will tend to be:

- Calm – laid back yet motivated and energized
- Confident – strong self-esteem but not arrogant
- Likeable – but not needy

- Honest – but not blunt
- Open – sharing but not self-indulgent
- Trustworthy – honourable but not a pushover
- Respectful – respects others as much as themselves
- Assertive – but not aggressive
- Positive – a can-do attitude but realistic.

They will also have:

- Sense of purpose – focused but not rigid
- Humour – a good sense of humour but not silly.

COACHING SESSION 23

How authentic are you?

If you were to score yourself on a scale of 1–10, how would you rate each of these dimensions?

Calm	☐	Respectful	☐
Confident	☐	Assertive	☐
Likeable	☐	Positive	☐
Honest	☐	Sense of purpose	☐
Open	☐	Sense of humour	☐
Trustworthy	☐		

LANGUAGE PATTERNS

Language patterns involve the concept of whether someone is visual, auditory, kinaesthetic or neutral. We first explored this in Chapter 2. You can pick up which language pattern might work for your audience by paying attention to body language, eye-accessing cues and the words people use:

System	Signs	Words	Phrases
Visual	Look up Defocus or stare into the distance Sit or stand erect Talk quickly	Look See Focus Visualize Reflect Clarify Reveal Outlook Foresee Vision	The future looks bright A flash of inspiration Shed some light on the matter An illuminating remark I see what you mean Looking closely at the idea
Auditory	Tilt the head to one side as if listening Breathe in the middle of the chest Use their voice expressively Move rhythmically	Say Sound Hear Tell Discuss Listen Ask Talk	Talk it over In a manner of speaking Turn a deaf ear Ring the changes I'm hearing you loud and clear
Kinaesthetic	Look down Breathe low in the chest Have a relaxed posture with rounded shoulders Talk slowly Talk in a low-pitched voice	Touch Solid Rough Grasp Gentle Hold Sensitive Hot Impact	I will be in touch A firm foundation Hold on for a second Let me grasp the point Too hot to handle I can't put my finger on it
Neutral	Look down	Think Consider Know Recognize Decide Logic	Think about it Consider the options I understand Do you agree?

This can be quite easy on a one-to-one basis, but complex in a group situation. If you have a large audience, most people will be visual so you can use a lot of visual language, and then pepper other language patterns through it. If you know the decision maker is neutral and, above all else, you must persuade them, opt for neutral language with the others peppered in.

- For example, for a mainly visual audience: 'If we focus (V) on a bright (V) future, listen (A) to each other, be sensitive (K) to each other's needs, logically (N) it follows that our two departments will have a positive outlook (V).'

- For a mainly neutral audience: 'If we think (N) about how we can work better together, talk (A) more, consider (N) each other's needs and put a logical (N) plan in place, I envisage (V) a firm foundation (K) for our two departments.'

There may be other words or acronyms people use, specific to their company or profession, which could be adopted to positive effect.

LANGUAGE OF INFLUENCE

In her book *Words that Change Minds*, Shelle Rose Charvet demonstrates using motivation and work traits how simple rephrasing can make all the difference between rapport and dissonance, acceptance and rejection.

Below you will see pairs of traits and how they differ. They are on a continuum, which means that people can vary in the degree to which they adopt one style or another. Underneath each pattern is an explanation of each trait and, in bold, specific language patterns that can be used to influence them.

For example, in the first pair, we have 'Towards' and 'Away from'. 'Towards' people are goal oriented and, as such, will want your language to be the same. 'In order to achieve ...' will work very well for them.

In contrast, an 'Away from' person who is risk averse will want to know what they can avoid in the achievement of the goal.

Let's take this a step further:

- **Towards** In order to achieve our sales target we need to ...

- **Away from** In order to avoid missing our target we need to ...

The general message is the same but their ability to harness buy-in from your audience will be quite different.

Towards	Away from
Knows what they want Thinks goals, not consequences **In order to achieve**	Thinks about consequences, risk averse, knows what they don't want **In order to avoid**
Internal	External
Knows within self if they've done a good job **What do you think? You might want to consider ...**	Needs feedback from others **So and so thinks, the feedback you will get is ...**
Necessity	Possibility
Needs structure, uses should and must **You should ...**	Likes choice, options, possibility **You could ...**

Specific	General
Likes detail and certainty **Exactly, precisely, specifically** ⟷	Likes big picture, sees connections **Essentially, the important thing is ...**

Similarity	Difference
Wants status quo, notices how things are alike, doesn't like change, not good on analysis **This is the same as before, the only difference ...** ⟷	Likes change, new ideas, revolution, good on analysis **This is a completely new way of doing things**

When you are able to integrate different styles into your presentation, you are in a much better position to influence. This presupposes you know your audience. However, they may be unknown to you. In this case you might want to think about the kind of organization they are. A firm of accountants is likely to be Away from, Internal, Specific and Similarity. A PR firm is likely to be Towards, External, Possibility, General and Difference. However, these are huge generalizations, and it is possible to be different in different contexts. Nevertheless, if you get this right you will notice a big difference in your message being accepted.

🗩🗩 COACHING SESSION 24

Using influencing language

In the following text, highlight which trait is represented and where. Look out for the following traits: Towards; Away from; Internal; External; Necessity; Possibility; Specific; General; Similarity; Difference.

If we are to achieve the results we want while avoiding the pitfalls associated with it, it's essential that we consider all the options, what could be done to achieve our vision and implement the detailed plan.

We'll still see quality output but what will be different will be the feeling of getting there more quickly and increasing our productivity.

You will know within yourselves and you will hear it from our customers – this plan will enable us to get to where we can be, where we need to be.

Think about it, see the evidence, hear the feedback.

Answer

If we are to achieve the results we want (Towards) while avoiding the pitfalls associated with it (Away from), it's essential (Necessity) that we consider all the options (Possibility), what could be done to achieve our vision (General, Visual) and implement the detailed plan (Specific).

We'll still see quality output (Similarity, Visual) but what will be different will be the feeling of getting there more quickly and increasing our productivity (Difference, Kinaesthetic).

You will know within yourselves (Internal) and you will hear it from our customers (External, Auditory) – this plan will enable us to get to where we can be (Possibility), where we need to be (Necessity).

Think about it (Neutral), see the evidence (Visual and External) hear the feedback (Auditory and External).

In addition, it is useful to consider in what way your audience is convinced. There are numerous convincer strategies that people adopt. When you know the decision-making approach of your audience, you can build that in to your presentation. Here are some:

Convincer strategies

- Number of examples
- Automatic
- Period of time Trusted source
- Logic/evaluation of the facts
- Gut/emotion
- Impact on bottom line

- Past record
- Tried and tested
- Endorsed by respected person
- Authority
- Cynics – constant need to re-evaluate - cynics are never completely convinced

COACHING SESSION 25

Who do you need to influence?

Think about an upcoming presentation you have to make and the key person you need to influence. Are they:

Auditory	☐
Visual	☐
Kinaesthetic	☐
Neutral	☐

Towards	☐	Away from	☐
Internal	☐	External	☐
Necessity	☐	Possibility	☐

Specific ☐　　　General ☐
Similarity ☐　　　Difference ☐

How are they generally convinced:
Number of examples ☐
Automatically ☐
Over time ☐
Through a trusted source ☐
Gut feel ☐
Impact on the bottom line ☐
Past record ☐
Tried and tested ☐
Endorsed by a respected person ☐
Authority ☐
Cynical ☐

Given all of this, how are you going to change your presentation?

EYE CONTACT

One of the principle ways of gaining rapport in a presentation situation is to practise good eye contact. It is tempting to focus on a friendly face in the audience, or a familiar face in a sea of strangers, or perhaps the person who just asked you a question. However, this kind of eye contact loses everyone else and will reveal your nervousness to your audience. Here are some eye contact tips:

- Your eyes should be gentle, not set and hard unless you need to be very assertive in your presentation.

- You shouldn't be staring.

- In answering a question, acknowledge the question and the individual with eye contact, then answer the entire room, coming back to the questioner periodically.

- You should punctuate your eye contact with glances away. In normal conversation, it is usual to look away as you contemplate a particular point. If this is done in a thoughtful way, rather than as though you are looking for something or someone more interesting, this can really enhance your rapport.

- Instead of sweeping the room with your eyes, focus on the eyes of individuals in each part of the room. In this way, everyone feels as though you have 'seen' them.

- If you are using a friendly face as a positive anchor (see Chapter 9), do make sure that you also look at others around the room as well.

HONOURING VALUES

What values does your audience hold? Values are what they consider to be important. These are often articulated on a company's brochure or website. Microsoft declare theirs in the following way (values are highlighted in bold):

'As a company, and as individuals, we value **integrity**, **honesty**, **openness**, **personal excellence**, **constructive self-criticism**, **continual self-improvement**, **and mutual respect**. We are committed to our customers and partners and have a passion for **technology**. We **take on big challenges**, and pride ourselves on **seeing them through**. We hold ourselves **accountable** to our customers, shareholders, partners, and employees by **honouring our commitments**, providing **results**, and striving for the **highest quality**.'

When you understand the values of your audience – whether it is a department or a whole company – it is possible to match their values in your talk. For example: 'You have our **commitment** that we will provide the **highest quality** product on time (**honouring commitments**). We want you to get the **results** you are looking for, so we are **open** to hearing from you about any modifications you may want. We believe this fits in perfectly with our culture of **excellence** and **continuous improvement**.'

PACING AND LEADING

In Chapter 7, when we discussed outcomes and structure, we discussed the importance of looking at what emotion you would like to create in your audience. To take this one step further, it may be helpful to think of what feelings they may be experiencing currently and the path they may need to take to get to where you want them to be. Let's say that you would like them to feel enthusiastic, but at the moment they feel cynical. A jump from cynicism to enthusiasm might be too much to expect to achieve in one fell swoop. However, the following may be more achievable:

Cynicism

↓

Curiosity

↓

Openness

↓

Enthusiasm

 COACH'S TIP

Pacing and leading

Simply being enthusiastic in your presentation is unlikely to convert the cynics who are likely to hold onto their position more strongly as a defence and/or counterbalance. However, if you pace and lead them, they are more likely to follow.

Pace

Pace can be considered metaphorically as 'walking alongside' your audience, acknowledging their reality, being where they are and understanding their hopes, fears and values. In addition it is using their language, their patterns. The purpose of pacing is to build rapport.

For example:

- John is quiet and reflective. If your presentation is loud and does not give enough time for reflection, John is likely to be left behind. You will have to work very hard at getting him on board.

- Eve talks quickly, thinks quickly and decides quickly. When you speak to her, it is important to match her to build rapport. If you are slow and indecisive, she is likely to switch off.

- Alex is concerned about the changes that you are proposing. Simply saying they are a good idea and he should get onside quickly is unlikely to raise the level of reassurance you need to help him perform at his best as quickly as you would like.

- Marion is feeling cynical because she has heard these promises before. Simply telling her it will be different this time is unlikely to transform her thinking.

In order to pace effectively, think about:

- What's important to them?

- Are they visual, auditory, kinaesthetic or neutral?

- Which traits do they have? (i.e. Towards, Away from, etc)

Lead

Once you have paced the audience and gained rapport, it is possible to lead them to where you want them to be. So, let's assume you have a cynical bunch and you want them to move towards enthusiasm. How might you do this?

Here is an example:

- **Pace their cynicism** 'I know you are wondering how on earth we can implement this new database by the end of the quarter and whether it really will speed up our response times. I too have wondered if it will actually create more problems than it solves. Given the year we have had, the last thing we want is another failed software system. We just don't have the capacity to weather another storm.'

- **Lead them into curiosity** 'So, **I wondered** whether the software provider had any experiences with companies like our own that have a complicated product offering across different continents and the different languages that we have to employ. **I was curious** as to how people in our shoes had experienced this change, what problems they had experienced and how they had overcome them.'

- **Lead them into openness** 'I found not one, not two, but three companies that had recently experienced this for themselves and could **be honest and open** about their experiences. To be **honest**, one of the companies didn't have such an **easy** time: they had not planned well in advance and they had decided to cut the training down from two weeks to just one. They paid the price. The other two companies had a **positive** experience – they liaised with the providers on the **best possible** implementation plan, including how, when and where the training should take place. The only person who struggled across the two businesses was one single new-hire who was entirely new to the business. They are up to speed now but it took an extra few weeks **understandably**. Everyone else has had a **positive experience**. Not simply with the **implementation** but with the **benefits of the new system:** You get the same results, but they are **easier, quicker**, with interdepartmental access so you are bothered less by the niggly questions that took up so much time in this old system we currently have.'

- **Lead them into enthusiasm** 'They were all **extremely enthusiastic** about the new software and just wish they had implemented it sooner. And, to make sure I was not just getting the managers' perspectives, I spoke to a good number of end-users and they were, to a man – and of course woman – **enthusiastic about this change**.

  I had already decided that if I did not have the **thumbs up** from them, I would not be **proposing it to you now**.'

- **Gain commitment** 'So, are you with me on this?'

You will notice that it leads them through the experiences of third parties. This is stronger than saying 'You will feel open when you see ...'. Nobody is fooled by this, but they are persuaded more easily by the social proof that this represents, in line with one of Robert Cialdini's influencing principles (see Chapter 7).

EASY VERSUS DIFFICULT

You will also notice that the word 'easy' was highlighted above. This was in reference to the company 'not having such an easy time'. This is a different way of saying that they had a difficult time. However, the use of the term 'easy' makes the difficulty seem less so. This is because the mind does not process negatives very well. When it hears 'not easy' it deletes the negative and only processes 'easy', as a general rule. When the mind hears the word 'difficult' it is under no illusion. When it hears 'not difficult' it only hears 'difficult'. Use this principle to work in your favour.

USE PAUSES TO EMPHASIZE POINTS

A lot of people believe that they must speak continuously, or they do so out of nerves and the desire to get it over with. This misses a very important opportunity as the use of pauses can create a powerful emphasis where you need it. Consider the following examples:

- 'We cannot continue as we are however if we take a stand now we can turn things around.'

- 'We cannot continue as we are ... However ... If we take a stand now ... we can turn things around.'

In the first example, it is difficult to absorb the gravitas of the message. It just feels like a stream of consciousness and has no real impact. Compare that to the second example. Here, the speaker uses strategic pauses to enable the audience to absorb each part of the message. It creates a 'cliff-hanger' for the next part so people hang on to every word. It is both easier to digest and has a stronger ability to influence.

CREDIBILITY VERSUS SYMPATHY

It can be tempting when you are nervous to appeal to the sympathies of the audience with comments such as:

- 'I'm sorry to take your time today.'
- 'I only got the call yesterday so apologies if my presentation isn't as polished as I'd like it to be.'
- 'Do forgive me. I haven't done a presentation before.'
- 'The baby kept me awake last night so apologies if I make any mistakes.'

Comments such as these may gain you sympathy from the audience but they can undermine your message and your credibility. Never, never, never go for the pity vote – you will find it practically impossible to be authoritative at the same time.

CREDIBILITY VERSUS APPROACHABILITY

Words account for only 7 per cent of how your message is perceived, with voice accounting for 38 per cent and body language 55 per cent. This section will focus on how to use your voice and body language to create a credible or approachable message.

There will be times when approachability is more important than credibility and vice versa. Michael Grinder, brother of the founder of NLP, covers this in his book *Charisma* and the main concepts are captured below.

- Credibility is important if you want to *deliver* an important message.
- Approachability is important when you want to *invite* input.
- To be credible, the head will be still, the palms down. At the end of the sentence your voice will drop and your head will lower.
- To be approachable, the head will nod, the palms will be up. At the end of the sentence your voice will rise and your head will rise to match it.

The following table describes the attributes of each style.

	Credible	Approachable
Listening: Head	Still	Bobs
Listening: Voice	Silent	Uh huh
At the end of a statement: Head	Down	Up
At the end of a statement: Voice	Drops	Lifts
Palms	Down	Up
Weight	Evenly distributed	More weight on one leg
Useful for	Sending information	Seeking information

Imagine the following sentence with both styles:

'I am your boss and I want your feedback. Who wants to go first?'

Your choice in which style to adopt makes all the difference in whether you achieve the feedback and whether that feedback is honest, or just what your audience thinks you would like to hear.

Here is a good pattern if you want to elicit input:

Do	Say
Palms up	Good afternoon (smile with softness around the eyes)
Lift voice at end, soft tone	I know I'm your boss
Drop voice at end	and I want **your** ideas (smile and softness around the yes)
Palms up and widen distance between them	Who wants to go first?

Here is a good pattern if you want to make a serious message:

Do	Say
Palms facing down	Good afternoon
Drop voice at the end	As the managing director
Drop voice at the end	I want to make an announcement
Drop voice at end and point to the slide	As you can see from this slide, we are not going to make our numbers this year

To distance yourself from a negative message and provide a more hopeful or positive one:

Do	Say
With head down, move away from the slide (separates you from negative message)	–
Lift head to neutralize the message, voice down, raise hands with palms down	I want to make some suggestions
Move away from negative slide onto flipchart with new information, voice down at the end of the sentence, hand palm down	To begin our recovery plan, I need you to …

MAKING A BUSINESS CASE

There will be times when you need to convince someone to take a specific course of action that they might be reluctant to take. This could be when an investment is required and your audience needs to be convinced of the return on their investment.

COACHING SESSION 26

Making a business case

There are several points to consider in making a business case:

1. Clarify what it is you want to do.

2. What are the benefits of doing this?

3. What are disadvantages of doing this? (This will help you flush out and deal with any possible objections beforehand.)

4. What are the disadvantages of staying with this status quo? (This will support your case.)

5. Who are the stakeholders? Consider the people who might be affected both positively and negatively by your proposal:

   a. Customers

   b. Suppliers

   c. Peers

   d. Other departments

   e. Directors

   f. Shareholders

   g. Employees

   h. Direct reports

6. Consider the impact to each of the stakeholders. For the positives, look at how to increase the effect of these. For the negatives, make recommendations about how to mitigate or guard against these. The individuals most negatively affected by your proposal will be the ones who are most likely to sabotage it for you so do make sure that you consider their position, acknowledge it and make some solid recommendations on how to deal with the situation.

7. Outline your proposed implementation plan – what you propose to do and when and the resources you will need to achieve your plan. Think in terms of:

   a. Financial

   b. Headcount

   c. Systems

   d. Equipment

   e. Training

   f. Support and collaboration of other departments

8. Be completely clear on the cost-benefit analysis to each of your stakeholders and end on a powerful note.

In creating your business case, it is important to support your case with facts. If it is possible, capture the commitment and opinions of influencers before your presentation. In this way, you have your in-built support. In terms of potential detractors, help them to see the big picture rather than simply the impact on them. Of course, if there are benefits to them it is important to show that too.

Above all, be honest in acknowledging potential problems, otherwise it will look as though you have not thought things through. Your proposal may fail for this reason alone. And, in doing that, do make sure that you come up with potential solutions to those problems so that your audience can see the way ahead. Do end, as always, on a strongly positive note.

Remember that even failed projects can have a compelling business case, such as the NHS 111 concept in the UK. What seemed like a good idea – a non-emergency number for people needing medical help – was unsuccessful because of a 'disastrous rollout' according to the British Medical Association. This risked patient care – the precise purpose for the entire concept. So, when planning your business case, make sure you think through all of the potential risks and make appropriate contingency plans – you don't want to shine at the presentation only to be humiliated at implementation stage.

COACH'S TIP

Potential problems

Be honest in acknowledging potential problems, otherwise it will look as though you have not thought things through.

BENEFITS VERSUS FEATURES

A lot of people talk about features – the characteristics of a product – instead of their benefits. This is not nearly as effective as talking about what that feature will do for you. For a fan, the features may be:

- desk top
- three speed settings
- oscillating.

These are potentially meaningless to the customer until you consider what the features mean for them:

- desk top – cool air right where you need it
- three speed settings – choose the power that's right for you according to the temperature of the room
- oscillating option – enjoy that cool air around the room if you want to spread the love.

Do talk about the benefits of your proposal and not the features of it, otherwise you may simply be blinding them with science.

PROBLEMS VERSUS SOLUTIONS

There will be times when you need to talk about problems. Wherever possible offer solutions, unless the purpose of the presentation is to solicit input on how to deal with the problem. Do remember to use language appropriate to your audience as discussed earlier in the chapter.

AVOIDING INSERTS

When searching for the right word, it is common to use 'inserts' such as:

- **You know** I, you know, want to talk to you about the importance of language.

- **Sort of like** I want to, sort of like, talk to you about the importance of language.

- **Er, um** I, er, want to talk to you, um, about the importance of language.

- **Like** I, like, want to talk to you, like, about, like the importance, like, of language.

However, as you will see from the examples given, such inserts really undermine your message. If you do need a moment or two to find the right word, simply pause with a thoughtful expression. This appears considered and credible.

CREATIVE LANGUAGE

There are various ways you can bring your presentation to life using language.

Rhymes

You might want to think about using rhyming words to bring a bit of fun to your presentation. They can help you to punctuate titles, make impactful messages, or to create a series of slides around a common theme. For example:

Opening slide	Presentation creation – Making powerful presentations
Slide 1	Presentation preparation – Setting the foundations
Slide 2	Presentation desperation – Handling nerves
Slide 3	Presentation sensation – Making an impact
Closing slide	Presentation creation – Guaranteed to succeed

Synonyms

A synonym is a word or phrase that means the same as another word or phrase. These are useful to avoid too much repetition and can provide variety and interest.

For example:

- Baffle – confuse, deceive

- Hardworking – diligent, determined, enterprising, industrious.

The world 'presentation' can have a number of meanings, so you need to think of the meaning of the word in the context of your message before finding a suitable synonym:

Meanings of the word 'presentation' and their synonyms

Performance	Award	Report
Performance	Award	Report
Exhibition	Donation	Talk
Demonstration	Giving	Lecture
Appearance	Offer	Seminar
Arrangement	Bestowment	Speech
Staging	Bestowal	Address
Production	Benefaction	Allocution
Management	Contribution	
Exposition	Awarding	

By using the thesaurus feature of your word-processing software, you can come up with alternative ways of saying the same thing to avoid repetition. For example, compare:

'If you want your presentation to compare well with other presentations, you might want to do your presentation differently.'

with:

'If you want your performance to compare well with other presentations, you might want to stage it differently.'

Antonyms

An antonym, by contrast, is a word that has the opposite meaning to the word you are using.

For example, antonyms for the word 'good' include awful, dreadful, hard, hopeless, inferior, lousy, painful, rotten, severe, stale, terrible and tough.

If you want to create more options, you can look for the synonyms of the antonyms. In this way, you might check your thesaurus for the word 'inferior':

Meanings of the word 'inferior' and their synonyms

Mediocre	Lower	Junior
Mediocre	Lower	Junior
Lesser	Junior	Minion
Lower	Secondary	Subordinate
Substandard	Subordinate	Underling
Poorer	Subsidiary	Menial
Low-grade	Minor	
Second-rate	Subservient	

Compare the following:

'It can be rewarding to be a good presenter. However, to avoid an inferior presentation, it's important to avoid inferior language patterns. In this way you will not appear inferior.'

with:

'It can be rewarding to be a good presenter. However, to avoid an inferior performance, it is important to avoid mediocre language patterns. In this way you will not appear second-rate.'

However, the following is even more powerful because of the use of the word 'inferior' twice in one sentence. It creates a more compelling case.

'It can be rewarding to be a good presenter. However, to avoid an inferior performance, it is important to avoid inferior language patterns. In this way you will not appear second-rate.'

The key is to play around with your words, 'try them on for size' and see what combination has the better impact.

Alliteration

This uses the repetition of consonants to create impact:

- cool, calm and confident
- big, bold and bright
- short shrift.

The Rule of Three

This technique makes your speech more memorable and commanding. Consider the following well-known examples:

- 'Never, never, never in the field of human conflict ...' (Winston Churchill)
- *Location, Location, Location* (TV programme)
- Father, Son and the Holy Spirit (Religion)
- *The Good, The Bad and The Ugly* (Film)
- 'Friends, family, community' comes from Jamie Oliver's Ted Awards Speech (see 'Consolidating what you have learned') in which he also slaps his notes three times to emphasize a point.
- 'My sense, my hope, my belief' comes from Susan Cain's speech on The Power of Introverts (see 'Consolidating what you have learned').
- 'Free at last, free at last, thank God almighty, we are free at last' is from Martin Luther King in his 'I have a Dream' speech.

Oxymorons

This is the juxtaposition of ideas, such as 'if you are feeling run *down* and fed *up* ...', 'alone together' and, to paraphrase a funny line from the sitcom *Friends* 'a little bit pregnant'.

Quotations

Using quotations can help you make a difficult point without attributing it to yourself. This can be an effective way of making the point more acceptable and more difficult to refute. For example, 'Wayne Burgraff, the American philosopher, said "It takes one hour of preparation for each minute of presentation time", so if there is one take away you should get from this book, it is to prepare well.'

Litotes

A litote is an ironic statement for dramatic effect. A great example is used by Jamie Oliver in his award-winning Ted speech: 'Fact: Diet-related disease is the biggest killer in the United States, right now, here today. This is a global problem. It's a catastrophe. It's sweeping the world. England is right behind you, as usual.' This produces laughter in the audience but the point is not at all lost on them.

Power words

It is useful to use action-oriented words in your presentation to instil a sense of confidence in what you are saying and make your message more compelling, powerful and persuasive. Some examples are given below:

Accelerate	Decide	Implement	Manage
Accomplish	Define	Improve	Market
Acquire	Deliver	Increase	Measure
Activate	Determine	Influence	Mobilize
Adapt	Encourage	Inform	Negotiate
Approve	Enhance	Inspire	Obtain
Authorize	Ensure	Install	Organize
Build	Establish	Integrate	Originate
Campaign	Evaluate	Interact	Outperform
Collaborate	Focus	Introduce	Participate
Communicate	Formulate	Investigate	Perform
Conclude	Foster	Join	Persuade
Connect	Generate	Launch	Plan
Consolidate	Identify	Maintain	Prevent

Prioritize	Resolve	Solve	Update
Propose	Respond	Sort	Validate
Prove	Restore	Succeed	Value
Quality	Secure	Support	Verify
Recommend	Serve	Target	Yield
Reconcile	Share	Transform	
Represent	Simplify	Unite	

COACH'S TIP

Creative language

Do remember to use the thesaurus and check for synonyms and antonyms and other ways to add greater flexibility, interest and variety to your presentation.

THINGS TO AVOID

Jargon

What is understood by you may not be understood by the audience. Using jargon can cause confusion and, worse, alienate people. The term 'due diligence' may be obvious to you, but will it be clear to your audience? 'We will be evaluating the proposal prior to signing the agreement' may be easier to understand.

Slang

Slang can make you sound unprofessional and affect your credibility. For example, 'ace' does not sound as powerful as 'excellent'. However, it may be appropriate for the audience you are presenting to. Do always consider your audience and what will create the best impact in terms of rapport, understanding and credibility.

Clichés

Clichés are well-known expressions that can sound irritating or tired. A common one is 'at the end of the day'.

Acronyms

Avoid acronyms as not everyone understands them. An acronym is an abbreviation using the initial letters of the words of a phrase or series of words, for example, NHS (National Health Service) and NATO (North Atlantic Treaty Organization).

Although these are well-known acronyms, do not assume that your audience will understand yours if they are commonly used in your industry or profession, but not necessarily understood outside. Using acronyms can leave your audience trying to work out the meaning of the acronym rather than the meaning of your message.

Humour

The effective and elegant use of humour can create rapport, deepen listening and improve buy-in. However, it can be difficult to execute effectively (interesting choice of words!). It also requires excellent timing. It should not be used as a replacement for good content but to enhance it and should only be used if you are good at it. The good news is that it can be learned.

People's listening is heightened just after laughter – they hear more of what you say and take more away from it.

Humour comes from the element of surprise. Rather than tell jokes ('Have you heard the one about …'), think in terms of stories and retorts.

In telling stories, or making points, it is important to paint a picture for the audience. It should move along a predictable route and have a sudden change of direction, a twist that the audience is not expecting and which creates a laugh. So, how can you build your punchline into your story?

The triad structure is a useful way to plan your humour – yes, you have to plan your humour too. A triad is a set of three. This is how it works:

- The first and second lines should be 'straight' lines – they should follow along a fairly predictable path.
- The third line of your story should change direction and create the laughter.

Here it is in practice:

- Set up: There are three reasons you should read this book.
- First straight line: The first is that it has lots of great information.
- Second straight line: The second is that it has lots of useful checklists.
- Third line: And the third is that I won't let you leave until you do

To see the structure of delivering humour using this method in a best man's speech, see http://www.youtube.com/watch?v=aahaq60e7DQ by presentation trainer and comedian Alan Donegan.

Your humour needs to have a target but should not offend. What is the difference between someone taking offence, or not? For the most part, it is about how you deliver the punchline – your attitude should be caring and your intent should be to help. In addition, it should be clear to the audience that your intent is benign and this is best done if you have a smile on your face and a twinkle in your eye.

COACH'S TIP

Using humour

Ask yourself, is my underlying intention correct?

Also, your belief system needs to support you. If you have a belief system of 'They will hate me', it is highly unlikely that any attempt at humour will succeed. If you have a belief system of 'I am connected' with a spirit of playfulness, this will help you be at one with the audience. Alan Donegan says 'Your state is contagious'. So, if you want your audience to feel a certain way, you have to go there first. If you want them to feel pain, you need to feel it first; if you want them to feel happy, you need to go there first.

As with all good things, practice makes perfect. The comedians you see, even the improvisers, have created a toolkit of jokes and have practised them to the degree that they can deliver them in any given set of circumstance. Often improvisation is not improvisation at all – it just looks that way.

COACHING SESSION 27

Using humour

Think of at least ten straight lines and list them down the left-hand side of the table below. In the right-hand column list ten twists that could make someone laugh. Then build these into a triad and test it out on friends. Test and refine, test and refine, test and refine. A small laugh from your friends is likely to yield a bigger laugh from your presentation audience because they will not be expecting the punchline. Humour is all about the unexpected.

	Straight line	Twist
1		
2		

	Straight line	Twist
3		
4		
5		
6		
7		
8		
9		
10		

There will be moments when you spontaneously deliver an improvised joke that gets you a good laugh. Do write these down and practise delivering them in different scenarios. This helps you to perfect your observation and delivery techniques so your presentations can benefit from some marvellously 'spontaneous' humour. However, if in doubt, leave it out.

COACHING SESSION 28

Lines that have got me laughs

Keep a note of any lines that have caused laughs and practise them in different scenarios.

THE VOICE OF INFLUENCE

Your voice tone accounts for 38 per cent of your message, so the quality of your voice is also incredibly important. Your voice needs to be congruent with your message and your body language.

Your voice also needs to project but not overpower. You don't want to have people recoiling at the sound or straining to hear you.

Breathing is the foundation of good speaking skills and, according to presentation and voice coach Constance Lamb, takes about five weeks to master. Most people speak on the held breath, particularly when nervous, instead of the outward breath. However, the breath really does the work for you – it gives life to your words.

By practising diaphragmatic breathing you will significantly improve the quality of your voice. Your diaphragm is a muscle located between your chest and your stomach. When you breathe deeply into your lungs, your stomach will expand naturally and your diaphragm will act as a kicker to propel the breath out.

Most people send their voice up to project it, but it needs to go down into the soles of your feet to project effectively.

Here are some voice tips for you:

- Place your feet firmly on the floor so that you feel grounded and strong. Then breathe and speak from your solar plexus on your outbreath. Really own your words.

- Avoid the antipodean lift which makes a sentence sound like a question. Compare the following:
    - This is really important?
    - This is really important.

- Which has more impact?

- Avoid the end-of-sentence wither that makes you sound either bored or unconfident, neither of which will endear you to your audience. Your voice should be strong.

- If possible, practise in the space you will be speaking in. Test the acoustics and claim the space so you can use it as if it is your front room and you are having a chat. This creates a level of intimacy, rapport and connection.

- Be aware of the 5Ps (see below).

The 5Ps

Pace This is the speed at which you speak. Too fast and people won't be able to keep up. Too slow and they will become bored. You can also change pace within the speech to create variety and texture.

Pitch This is the quality of the sound of your voice, the rise and fall of the tone and the volume. Again, variety is important. If you are talking about something exciting you might want to raise your voice; for something more serious, you might want to lower it. A sentence should sound like a melody with a natural modulation in tone and rhythm.

Also think about whether you want certain words to stand out. You can do this easily with your voice tone (and the pause – see below). For example, try reading out the following sentence by emphasizing different parts of it each time you repeat it. Notice how it changes the meaning of the sentence completely:

1. **I** really like presenting.

2. I **really** like presenting.

3. I really **like** presenting.

4. I really like **presenting**.

The first example implies that, of all the people present, you are the one who likes presenting or that you disagree with those who don't like it.

In the second example, you are emphasizing the extent of your enjoyment of presenting.

The third example is a simple statement of how you feel about presenting.

The fourth example indicates that presenting is one of the things you enjoy as distinct from other activities.

What you choose to emphasize can really alter your message in subtle yet profound ways. Remember that the voice accounts for 38 per cent of how your message is received.

Projection This is the power of your voice. It is not the same as volume. Projection is required so that your voice will carry to the far reaches of the room. If you are feeling nervous, it is easy to 'swallow' your voice, making it difficult for you to be heard.

If you practise diaphragmatic breathing (see above) and imagine laying the words on your breath, this will carry your voice for you. It is helpful to imagine projecting your voice into the next room if you feel it doesn't have sufficient strength. For most people, the effect will be that the voice carries comfortably around the room in which you are presenting, though it may *feel* like you are shouting if you are unused to this.

Pause Pauses are very effective in creating drama, delivering a punchline and also in providing punctuation. Punctuation is important for clarity and understanding and to enable the audience to absorb what has been said.

Precision Clarity in your diction – making sure you articulate your words clearly – is also important for your speech. Practising tongue twisters can improve your diction enormously. Here are some for you to enjoy practising with:

Peter Piper picked a peck of pickled peppers
Did Peter Piper pick a peck of pickled peppers?
If Peter Piper picked a peck of pickled peppers,
Where's the peck of pickled peppers Peter Piper picked?

Red lorry, yellow lorry, red lorry, yellow lorry.

Betty Botter had some butter
'But,' she said, 'this butter's bitter.
If I bake this bitter butter,
It would make my batter bitter.
But a bit of better butter –
That would make my batter better.'
So she bought a bit of butter,
Better than her bitter butter,
And she baked it in her batter,
And the batter was not bitter.
So 'twas better Betty Botter
Bought a bit of better butter.

She sells sea shells by the sea shore.
The shells she sells are surely seashells.
So if she sells shells on the seashore,
I'm sure she sells seashore shells.

You've no need to light a night-light
On a light night like tonight,

For a night-light's light's a slight light,
And tonight's a night that's light.
When a night's light, like tonight's light,
It is really not quite right.

A Tudor who tooted a flute
Tried to tutor two tooters to toot.
Said the two to their tutor,
'Is it harder to toot
Or to tutor two tooters to toot?'

Have fun with these two!

I slit the sheet, the sheet I slit, and on the slitted sheet I sit.

I am not the pheasant plucker,
I'm the pheasant plucker's mate
I am only plucking pheasants
'Cause the pheasant plucker's late.

YOUR APPEARANCE

You are your own visual aid. How you look will either support or detract from what you have to say. Do think about your audience, your message and the culture as you plan what to wear. Your appearance needs to fit the occasion. If in doubt go for more formal and conservative. Your appearance will not only help you feel more confident but also help your audience feel more confident in you.

Check the finer details of what you are wearing:

- Audience and situation appropriate
- No missing buttons, loose threads or droopy hems
- Suits should not be shiny
- Clothing should be clean and well pressed

- No clashing colours or patterns (checked shirt, spotty tie and a pinstripe suit will give people headaches)
- Shoes well-polished and price stickers removed
- Hosiery free from ladders, holes or bobbly bits
- Clothes lint free
- Hair and hands well-groomed
- Flies and buttons done up (no chest hair or cleavage)
- Discreet jewellery
- Well applied make-up
- If you tend to sweat, do wear clothes that are cool and do not show sweat.

 COACH'S TIP

Your appearance

If your outfit and grooming make you feel confident, it is likely to have hit the right note.

You cannot antagonize and influence at the same time.

John Knox

→ NEXT STEPS

In this chapter you have learned about the nature and importance of rapport in achieving your outcome with your presentation, together with various ways of doing this including the art of language. You have looked at how to pace and lead your audience from one emotional state to another so that you have them in the palm of your hands. You have discovered when you need to be credible or approachable and how to achieve this in the use of your voice and your body language. You have explored the elements of presenting a business case and how to distinguish between a feature and a benefit. To add an element of enjoyment for your audience you have looked at how to be creative with your language and how to use humour effectively. Finally, you have revisited the use of your voice and the importance of your appearance to create an impact.

In the next chapter you will learn about the practical preparations and considerations for your presentation.

TAKEAWAYS

This is your opportunity to take stock of what you have learned from this chapter. You might want now to choose other chapters and exercises to focus on, or you can continue to work through the whole book if this fits your needs more.

Think about a presentation you recently saw which had a surprising impact on you. Which techniques did they employ which had the best effect on you?

How did they use humour? Was it effective or not? Why?

How effective were they in the employment of the 5Ps?

Which three strategies in this chapter will give you the biggest improvement in your ability to engage and influence your audience?

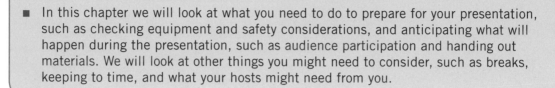

PRACTICAL PREPARATIONS AND CONSIDERATIONS

OUTCOMES FROM THIS CHAPTER

- In this chapter we will look at what you need to do to prepare for your presentation, such as checking equipment and safety considerations, and anticipating what will happen during the presentation, such as audience participation and handing out materials. We will look at other things you might need to consider, such as breaks, keeping to time, and what your hosts might need from you.

There are certain practicalities that need to be considered when preparing your presentation, whether it is a simple presentation in a familiar place to a small audience, or a presentation where you are one of several speakers to a large audience.

BEFORE YOUR PRESENTATION

Equipment

You need to check what equipment is available to you before you decide how you want to present. There are a number of presentation aids available to you, from very low-tech to the latest technology. It may be that you want to present without any. To do this, you need to really be able to work the floor and be highly confident in yourself and in your content. Presentation aids help you to keep on track and to support your message. Check out Chapter 8 for more information on what is available. Remember that as people absorb information using a variety of senses, it is always useful to present it using the different senses wherever possible (see Chapter 10).

You should make sure that your presentation is relevant for about 80 per cent of your audience.

Know your numbers

How many people will be attending? This is important so that you know how many handouts to produce and how to design your feedback sessions appropriately. Running a brainstorming session with a group of 50 from the front of the room will be practically impossible. However, splitting people into groups to come up with a consolidated list and having them call out their answers to the front will be simpler. Audience numbers will also dictate room layout (see below).

Order of play

If you are one in a series of presenters, consider where you will be in the order of play. Are you just after lunch? First on? Last on? Who do you follow? Does that person have a very positive or very negative message that has implications for your own presentation? Do you need to make accommodations in how you position your talk?

Room layout

Think about how you want the room to be laid out, though this may already be dictated by the event.

Boardroom style	This is a solid table with you at one end, presenting, and everyone else sitting around the table. This limits the numbers you can present to.
Theatre style	This has you at the front, usually on a stage, with everyone seated in rows in front of you. You can usually fit in a lot of people using this style.
U-shape	This has a bank of tables leading down from your right, across and up to your left so that they create a U-shape with you at the open end.
Classroom style	This is a bank of desks neatly arranged in front of you.
Banquet style	This is a series of round tables with you at the front, usually on a stage.

These layouts vary in degrees of formality, the numbers that can be accommodated and the ease with which you can interact with the audience.

Audience participation decisions

It is useful to decide in advance in what way, if at all, you would like to include or involve your audience. Whether you do or don't, your audience may have questions during your presentation and it is useful to consider what these might be in advance, and how you would like to handle them.

Questions can be very useful in making some of your points but they can interfere with the flow of your presentation if they are not managed well.

Decide in advance if you want questions at the end of your presentation or if you are happy to accept them during the presentation.

Breaks

Think about how you want to manage breaks during your presentation – do you want to make yourself available to the audience or do you want to take time out for yourself. This is a personal decision. Making yourself available allows you to answer questions people might feel too embarrassed to ask in front of everyone. It also gives you time to create more rapport and get feedback. However, it may be that you need to gather your thoughts and conserve your energy for the next part of your presentation. Decide in advance how you will manage breaks.

Spell check

Remember to spell-check your presentation – there is nothing like undermining your credibility with spelling errors, whether this is in your handout or your slideshow. And, with spell-checker, there are no excuses. However, it is dangerous to rely solely on spell-checker, as a word might be spelled correctly but is not the word you are looking for. To safeguard against this, ensure you read through everything several times over.

Decide when to give handouts

Always have hard copies of your presentation available for your audience. Not only does this help if your computer suddenly crashes, it also helps engage people on the kinaesthetic level – they can engage with your presentation using the sense of touch which can enhance their interest and absorption of the material. However, when should you give these out?

- **At the beginning** This means they will be able to follow what you say as you go along. The downside is that they may look ahead.

- **As you go** If you give handouts as you go, this stops the audience from looking ahead, which means they are focusing on what you are saying. However, it can be quite disruptive passing round handout after handout.

- **At the end** You can decide to distribute your handouts at the end of your presentation. However, some people might get very upset if they are not provided with the means of taking notes. They may take their own notes anyway, which means they are spending even more time writing than they might otherwise have spent if you had just passed the handouts round in the first place.

 COACH'S TIP

Caution

Some speakers ask their audience not to make notes because handouts will be given at the end, but then the handouts are clearly lacking some of the detail the audience might have liked to have noted down. This leaves you with a disgruntled audience. Do tell your audience what will be included in the handouts and what is excluded so that they know what notes to take themselves.

Different types of handouts

There are various ways that you can produce handouts for your audience. Following are a selection for you to choose from:

1. Your own typed notes.

2. Copies of slides:

   - 1 to a page: takes a lot of ink and leaves no room to write
   - 2, 3, 4, 6, 9 to a page: think about what you want the handouts to achieve and whether it will help them do that. Printing notes this way leaves little room to write notes and can be difficult to read
   - Handouts: three slides to a page with space for notes alongside

3. Notes pages. These have one slide per page with any notes you have written underneath. However, these notes pages are not normally intended for the use of your audience so do think carefully whether it is the way to go for you.

What do your hosts need?

Think about what your host needs from you if you are part of an event organized by someone else:

- Title of presentation
- Summary
- Bio
- Specific requirements, i.e. equipment, layout, water, etc.
- Will they set up for you or are you required to do this yourself?

Once you have submitted your information, don't make any changes as it will likely have been used in their promotional material so people's expectations will have been set.

Practice

There is nothing like practice to prepare you. If you can, do this in front of a video, or perhaps a full-length mirror. This enables you to capture any unfortunate mannerisms and tics and correct them. It also helps you to become one with your presentation so that you are natural on the big day.

Another tip is to practise in the room where you will be presenting. This allows you to check out the acoustics, where you want to stand, where the equipment should go and whether people will be able to hear you and see you at the back of the room.

Practise it right the way through so that you know you can deliver your presentation, with questions, in the time allocated. It can be quite irritating to your audience if you overrun as they might have trains to catch or somewhere else to be. Do not be seduced by a seemingly engaged audience – they can still become irritated if you overrun or cut them short, leaving out important elements of your message, or not giving people enough time to ask some relevant questions to aid their understanding.

Do critique yourself using the checklist in Appendix 2 at the end of the book. There are three rules to be mindful of:

1. Practise and refine.

2. Practise and refine.

3. Practise and refine.

Just in case

- Make sure that you bring your own marker pens as they often go missing or do not write clearly.

- Bring hard copies of your presentation, including your own notes, just in case the technology lets you down at the last minute.

- If you are not familiar with the venue, you might want to bring your own power cable as the last thing you want is be fully prepared but not able to show your presentation because of a simple technicality.

- Have your presentation on a memory stick as an extra backup.

Be familiar with the room/setting

- It is important for you to feel comfortable with the space in which you will be presenting. If possible, check it out before the day.

- Check that people at the back of the room can see and hear your presentation once the room is full and you are miked up.

- Does the lighting work for you? Does the room have dimmer switches? Does the light from the window mean that the presentation will be difficult to see? Do the windows have blinds you can use? Find out where the controls are, which lights should be switched on, which dimmed, etc.

- Are the temperature and ventilation suitable? Where are the controls if you need to make adjustments?

- Where should the flipchart and the projector be positioned to create optimum visuals? Do be careful about trailing wires – you don't want any accidents on your big day.

COACH'S TIP

Test all the equipment

Check all the equipment before your talk, leaving plenty of time for troubleshooting if necessary.

Microphone practice and tips

Some presentations will require that you use a microphone so that you can be heard. Here are some useful tips to help you:

- Remember to switch it on.

- Learn how to position the microphone in front of your mouth to get the right effect.

- Make sure that you maintain that distance between your mouth and the microphone – avoid turning your head with the microphone in place because it will not pick up your voice.

- About 15–20 cm is usually the right distance – more than this and you will start to pick up other sounds around the room like cutlery cluttering and children crying if you are at a wedding. Closer than this and you will start 'p-popping' your p's.

- Do a sound check before people start arriving so that you are familiar with how much or little power to use in your voice.

- Keep the microphone firmly in your hand – if you slip or change your grip, the sound will come through and interfere with your speech.

- Types of microphone:

    - podium-based – you stand in one position

    - on a stand – raise or lower it to your own height, detachable if you want to move around

    - lapel microphone – leaves both hands free but you need to be aware of keeping your head positioned close to the microphone.

COACH'S TIP

Safety considerations

Make sure cables are secure and there are no trip hazards either for you or for members of your audience.

Getting there

Build in contingency time to make sure that you arrive on time, bearing in mind possible traffic/transport delays, time to find a parking space, queue for your train ticket, getting petrol, unloading the car, setting up.

COACHING SESSION 29

Estimating time

Complete the table below to ensure you have sufficient time for everything you need to do.

Estimated time	
Travel to venue (consider whether rush hour or not)	
Train/traffic delays (be generous)	
Buying petrol (with queue)	
Queue for train ticket	
Loading car for departure	
Unloading car on arrival	
Car park to reception to meeting room (allow for long walk and reception queues)	
Setting up	
Total estimated time to presentation	

Even if you are presenting at your place of work, allow time for people stopping you in the corridor to ask an important question.

It is always good to arrive in plenty of time in order to relax before your presentation so you feel grounded and resourceful.

Arriving at the venue

If you are one of many speakers on the day and you are in any way visible to the audience while other participants are presenting, do make sure you appear attentive, interested, calm and in control. People will start to make their opinions about you before your turn to speak, so this is time well spent.

If you arrive early, you might want to mingle with the audience and gain rapport with them prior to the presentation starting. However, if you prefer to be quiet with your own thoughts, it is better to be in an entirely different room so that you do not appear stand-offish or nervous.

COACH'S TIP

Get organized

Looking organized makes you feel organized. Feeling organized makes you look organized.

When you feel organized you have more confidence and can communicate with greater clarity. This will give more power and authenticity to your presentation.

Physical preparation to remove tension

- Take some deep breaths to calm yourself just before it's your turn.
- Do some gentle head rotations in both directions.
- Move your head gently backwards and forwards.
- Open your mouth and work your jaw to relax it.
- Relax your tongue and your mouth.
- Relax your forehead and scalp.
- Circle your shoulders to loosen them.
- Clench and unclench your hands a few times.
- Clasp your hands and flex your arms forward.
- Do the same flexing them behind you, feeling the tension in your arms.

Call of nature

It is perfectly normal to have an urgent need for the toilet prior to your presentation – this is a natural effect of the fight-flight response. Make a quick visit just before and you should be fine.

DURING YOUR PRESENTATION

Taking the stand

When you are finally called on stage, walk calmly and deliberately with your papers. Take a glass of water with you if one is not provided. Take your time as this helps to calm you and shows the audience you are in control. When you are finally on stage, again, take your time to assemble everything. This can build a positive anticipation with your audience if it is done with confidence.

On stage

As always, do make sure that your face is relaxed, your eyes soft and your expression open. Look at the audience as if they are friends you intend to help. This will create a stronger connection and help you to feel more in control.

Moving around the stage increases your audience engagement but keep it calm, natural and purposeful. This is not the time for nervous pacing.

Refer to your slides but don't read them. Point to an item of interest on a slide then look back at the audience. This links your talk to the presentation but means that the audience is focused on you.

Keeping to time

It can be tempting to look at your watch during your presentation to keep to time. However, this makes you look either bored or nervous, neither of which will do much for your credibility.

However, keeping to time not only makes you look like a professional but is respectful of the audience. They may have trains to catch, sitters to relieve or other meetings to get to.

In addition, you may be one in a long line of presenters that day – no one likes a hogger (see Chapter 12) and if you run late, that upsets everybody's schedule. This will not endear you to the organizers, your fellow-presenters or your audience.

It is worth remembering that everything you do in your presentation is saying something about you as a person – from what you say, to the way you dress and the way you behave. You are your own visual aid, marketing tool and referral generator. What would running over time say about you?

Aim to finish on time or sooner – that will give people more time for questions. People love to be given time to ask their questions rather than be rushed along.

However, if you finish too soon, that will leave you too much time and space to fill so it is a good idea to have some additional slides or material. For example:

■ 'As we have a little extra time ...'

■ 'You have grasped the concepts so well; I would like to share with you one more thought ...'

On the other hand, you might be at the mercy of audience members who like to hog the limelight, leapfrog from one subject to another or get too bogged down in one subject. Managing such individuals is very important and will be covered in Chapter 12.

To keep on schedule:

- Have your presentation schedule in front of you which shows how long each section should take.

- Have your watch next to it so it is easy to keep on track. You can also look at the clock on your laptop if you are using one, though your eyesight would need to be pretty good.

- You may want to call on a friendly member of the audience to indicate to you at various points during your presentation, either with pre-prepared signs, or by simply showing with their hands, how many minutes you have left. Be clear when you want indicators, e.g.:

    - 20 minutes left

    - 10 minutes left

    - 5 minutes left

    - 1 minute left.

- The downside of this method is that that person will be focused more on the time than on your presentation.

- Keep your eye on the wall clock. It is useful to position yourself so you can see it clearly.

> *The best preparation for good work tomorrow is to do good work today.*
>
> Elbert Hubbard

 NEXT STEPS

In this chapter you have learned about the practical considerations before and during your presentation so that it goes without a hitch. This includes deciding on the room layout, decisions about how you want to involve your audience, when to give handouts (and what type), managing breaks, how to prepare yourself for your presentation, how to use the microphone if appropriate, how to plan your entrance and how to keep to time. You have looked at the importance of familiarizing yourself with the room in which you will be presenting so that you feel comfortable in the space and to be aware of safety considerations. You have even looked at how to make sure you arrive at the venue on time given the various obstacles which can get in your way.

In the next chapter you will learn how to deal with the unexpected – those hecklers and hiccups which can threaten your presentation.

👍 TAKEAWAYS

This is your opportunity to take stock of what you have learned from this chapter. You might want now to choose other chapters and exercises to focus on, or you can continue to work through the whole book if this fits your needs more.

Thinking about an upcoming presentation. What room layout will best serve you?

Will handouts be appropriate? If so, what type? And, when do you plan on distributing them?

What will be the challenges of the environment in which you will be presenting?

How do you propose to deal with these?

12 EXPECTING THE UNEXPECTED

 OUTCOMES FROM THIS CHAPTER

- In this chapter we look at how to deal with things that go wrong so that your presentation is a success. This can range from hecklers, to dealing with difficult questions or a hostile audience, to making mistakes such as losing your place or even falling over.

When you plan for the unexpected and it happens, it doesn't derail you in the same way that the unprepared speaker may be affected. In fact, it can really improve your rapport and credibility if handled correctly. In this chapter, we will explore some useful techniques to help you handle problems with grace and ease.

What would cause anyone to heckle in the first place? They could be scoring points in front of another member of the audience, they may have some grievance, they may feel threatened or they may have a genuine question. Whatever the motivation for their behaviour, it is important to prepare for it and handle the situation with grace, dignity and respect. You will be judged on how you handle these situations, and these challenges, handled well, can really elevate you as an expert and a professional. Cherish these opportunities and learn from them. Listen with an open mind; avoid talking over interrupters or jumping to conclusions as this will simply alienate them further.

For the moment, here are some tips for you.

PREVENTION IS BETTER THAN CURE

If you prepare your subject well, know your presentation inside out and plan for the unexpected, you will feel more confident in your presentation and that you can handle anything. We handled the practicalities of preparation in the previous chapter. But, in case you have skipped through this book, if you haven't read about preparation before, please do read it before you go further.

As part of your preparation, think of different ways of looking at your subject. How would different people think about it? By preparing your perspective you will be more equipped to handle difficult questions. We dealt with this in Chapters 7 and 10.

START FROM A POSITION OF STRENGTH

Rule number 1 is not to take it personally. If you are thinking something along the lines of 'Don't shoot the messenger' or 'It isn't my fault' then these thoughts will make you feel vulnerable. Even a direct attack isn't necessarily personal.

So, having a genuine desire to understand and help will stand you in good stead. When you notice a negative thought, turn it around so that it develops understanding instead of confrontation. For example:

Negative thought	Possible alternative
Don't shoot the messenger	They are feeling threatened or sensitive
It isn't my fault	They need someone to blame

Once you have a new perspective, acknowledge the situation:

- 'I know you didn't want to hear this ... however, if we are to remain competitive in this market place, and have job security, this is important for each and every one of us.'

- 'It is true that we made some mistakes. What's important right now is that we start to learn from those mistakes and take actions to correct them.'

BE MINDFUL OF BODY LANGUAGE

If someone appears approving it is a good opportunity to harness this to support your case: 'That seems to have struck a chord with you Greg – would you like to say more about this?' Only do this if you want to invite further discussion.

If someone appears disapproving you could say: 'You seem to have concerns about that particular point – would you like to give your perspective on this Andrew?' This flushes out negativity with you in the driving seat.

LATE ARRIVALS

It is almost guaranteed that someone will arrive late. This should not derail you – it is important to be respectful to everyone in the room without drawing attention to the latecomer who may be embarrassed. To deal with it, here are a couple of options:

- Ignore them and carry on.

- Use humour: 'So that's the secret of (subject of your presentation). Any questions?' This usually gets a laugh.

PEOPLE HOLDING SIDE CONVERSATIONS

In large meetings, it is often the case that some individuals will start a conversation with their neighbour while you are talking. This can be distracting for you and for the other audience members. In order not to undermine yourself, it is important to deal with this kind of situation with as much grace as possible. Here are some strategies that may help:

- Walk around to the offending group and stand by them as you continue with your presentation. Your presence will interrupt their conversation whereupon you can simply smile, thank them, and continue.

- Lower your voice as you present. This will often cause the audience to refocus their attention on you.

- Say to the group: 'Could we have just one person speaking at once please.'

AWKWARD AND HOSTILE QUESTIONS

Some people make it their business to ask awkward questions. The trick is not to take it personally. Sometimes, the people who do this do so merely because they are intensely interested in what you are saying. Sometimes, it is because they want to be seen as your intellectual superior (this is usually a sign of vulnerability). Sometimes it is just a genuine question that simply feels uncomfortable to you.

One of the reasons that people are nervous about presenting is because they don't want to be seen as incompetent. The fact is that we are not going to know the answers to all the questions. It is perfectly acceptable, and actually desirable, to say that you don't know the answer. This increases your credibility if you say it in the right way. Pretending that you know is usually very transparent to the audience and can undermine your entire presentation. So, it's essential to be honest.

Here are some suggested responses:

- 'That's a great question Max. I don't have that answer here for you but will get back to you by tomorrow with a full response.'

- 'That's a great question Max and completely relevant though not my specialization. John, this is your area – do you have a response for Max?' (Only do this if you know John has the answer, otherwise it will look like you are trying to put John on the spot instead.)

- 'That's a great question Max. It requires more time than we have today. Can we take this offline?'

- 'Great question Max. However, I understand Peter is covering this in his presentation.'

- 'That's a great question Max. It requires more time that we have today. Can I suggest that we have a separate meeting to discuss it so that it gets the attention that it deserves?'

■ 'That's a great question Max. Let's put it on our Parked Issues Chart and come back to that if we have time at the end of the presentation.'

Avoid saying things like 'As I've already said ...' as this antagonizes. Always speak respectfully, no matter how provocative the situation.

COACH'S TIP

Difficult questions and answers

Do rehearse difficult questions and answers as much as possible so that you stay in control and are able to respond graciously.

YOU DON'T UNDERSTAND THE QUESTION

There will be times when someone asks a question that is very complex or perhaps hasn't been worded very well. Or maybe you were thinking about making your next point and weren't paying proper attention. This can be dealt with in the following ways:

■ 'I'm not sure I understood your question, could you repeat it please?'

■ 'I didn't quite hear your question, could you repeat it please?'

■ 'Could you expand on that please? I am not sure I understand what you are asking.'

Never, never, never belittle the questioner in any way. It will only reflect badly on you. Always be respectful and responsive. Always acknowledge their input and point of view, even though you may not agree with it.

THINKING TIME

If you need time to think of your answer, you would be surprised how a little time is a long time when it comes to it. We often think that any pauses must be filled but, actually, pauses can be usefully employed to give your mind time to think through what you want to say. For example:

■ Pause

'That's a great question Max.'

■ Pause

Repeat Max's question slowly.

■ Pause

'Now, let me think about that for a moment.'

- Pause

Your answer

This delaying tactic gives you time to find the answer you need.

If you still need more time, say 'That's a great question. I need to reflect on that – can I come back to you at the end of the presentation?' This is only helpful if you know you have the answer and just need a little time. If you don't actually know the answer, say so. People will respect you more for it.

NO QUESTIONS FORTHCOMING

If your presentation relies on questions and there aren't any forthcoming, try one of these strategies:

- If someone has asked you a good question concerning the subject prior to your presentation, you can refer to it: 'David asked me last week if this would impact the integration of the two departments and I would like to answer that question for all of you ...'

- If you want to make a general point: 'A question I am often asked is ...'

- Explain: 'Often the simplest questions create the greatest benefit to the group – most people are thinking exactly the same thing and so your questions will help others. Now's your chance.'

- 'In groups of three, I would like you to put together a list of the top three questions you have about what has been said so far.'

Give them time and space to come up with their questions and make sure your general demeanour is open and facilitative. Some people ask if there are any questions so quickly and brusquely, either through nerves or time pressures, that the effect is for the audience to clam up.

Asking questions requires that you be entirely focused on what the person is saying so that you can provide a full answer for the audience.

DIFFICULTY HEARING THE QUESTION

Sometimes, depending on the size and acoustics of the room, it may be necessary to repeat the question for the benefit of the audience: 'This lady is asking whether the new branch will be open by Christmas. Our plan is that it will be open four weeks beforehand so that we can take full advantage of the buying season. Does that answer your question?' (looking at lady kindly).

TOO MANY QUESTIONS

If you have a very tight schedule and you are worried that there will be too many questions which could disrupt your presentation, you might want to think about taking questions at the end. Ask your audience to make a note of their questions to ask during your Q&A session. The result will be that some people will forget to ask their question, others will find that your presentation answers their question after all, or that someone else asks their question for them. This technique needs to be balanced with the need for the audience to feel engaged and heard.

YOU DON'T AGREE WITH WHAT IS BEING SAID

There will be times when an audience member makes a point with which you don't agree. This can be tricky because it's important to be respectful while at the same time being authentic. Always validate what you can in the question before making your point:

- **Acknowledge** The purpose here is to acknowledge the individual's point without agreeing with it:
    - 'That's an interesting point of view Jo – I hadn't thought of it that way.'
    - 'I know this is really important to you Jo ...'
- **Redefine the problem** The purpose here is to acknowledge the point but provide another more important perspective on it. To a comment about someone not enjoying the course, you might state:
    - 'I think, Jo, that the issue is not whether you are finding the course difficult but how you will apply what you've learned from it.'
- **Use an agreement frame** The purpose here is to acknowledge the point and provide an expansion to the idea:
    - 'I understand that you think the course is quite difficult *and that means that* you are definitely broadening your skills.'
- **Use 'and' in place of 'but'** The purpose here is to transform a negative into a positive, e.g.:
    - 'I know you are finding the course difficult *but* I know its broadening your skills.' This negates what precedes the word 'but', making it a negative statement. Compare that to 'I know you are finding the course difficult *and* I know that it's broadening your skills.' This embraces both parts of the sentence and makes it more positive, thereby more influential.
- **Use 'yet'** Yet is a great process word that is used to address a comment which implies that the present is what it is and shows that all that is needed is time:

- 'I know that you haven't digested it all yet.'
- You can then add: 'You'd be surprised how much you are learning without even realizing it' to further the concept.

MANAGE HOGGING, FROGGING AND BOGGING

In this section we will be looking at how to manage the flow as affected by the audience. So, let's explore different strategies to help keep them on track.

Hogging

Every self-respecting audience will have a hogger who will want to dominate the proceedings. Either they like the limelight, have a point to prove or they are genuinely interested. However, in the interests of time and in fairness to other audience members, it is important to manage this situation. For example:

- **If they answer all the questions**: 'OK Steve, since you answered the last question, why don't we see if someone else would like to take this one?'
- **If they are the only one making comments**: 'OK Steve, you've made some excellent points. Let's see if someone else has any points they would like to make about this.'
- **If they take too long to answer**: 'Steve, that's a lot of information. Is it possible to give your answer in a couple of bullet points?'

Frogging

Frogging is about leapfrogging from one subject to another. This can be a sign of loss of focus or it could mean that you are generating lots of thought. Here is how you might want to handle these situations:

- 'Steve, we will be talking about this later in my presentation. For now, let's stick with ...'
- 'Thanks Steve. This is outside the scope of our discussion today. Shall we take it offline?'
- 'Great question Steve. Let me put that up on the Parked Issues Chart and see if we have time at the end to deal with it.'

Do keep your own answers short – you don't want to derail yourself!

Bogging

Getting bogged down in too much detail can risk you not getting through the material and it's important to think about the big picture: is it more important to go into the detail of this section, or to cover the breadth of your planned discussion in less depth? Think about your overall outcome – to what degree does this support or detract from your achievement of it? How will your audience react if you don't get through the original agenda? Here are some possible responses:

- 'I see that we have a lot to say about this subject. However, in order that we can go through everything else in the agenda, can I suggest that we make a separate meeting so that we can give this the attention it deserves?'

- 'I can see we have a lot to say about this subject. Can I take a vote about whether we spend more time on this today and leave the rest of the agenda for another meeting?'

- 'I can see that we have a lot to say about this subject. However, it's important that we go through the whole agenda so that you can see this subject in context so can I propose we move onto the next item?'

SQUIRMING, FIDGETING OR YAWNING AUDIENCE MEMBERS

People can absorb at a greater speed than they can speak. This means that your pace is important, as is making your presentation active so that you keep people engaged. If you are too slow they will zone out, but you need to give them space to process what you are saying too, so do punctuate with pauses.

Watch your audience for signs of in comprehension, boredom or annoyance so that you can adapt your presentation accordingly.

If you notice any squirming, fidgeting and yawning in your audience, it could simply be a sign of tiredness. Or, worse, boredom. One of the following should remedy the situation:

- Make sure your voice is well modulated – increase the speed if you are going too slowly.

- Ask the audience a question. This will engage their minds and increase their energy and focus.

- Change the energy – lean in and lower your voice to create more intimacy and engagement; increase your pace and voice to create excitement.

- Suggest a group activity – it is good to have some of these up your sleeve. These can either be additional activities in line with your presentation, or alternative ways of engaging your audience with your content. Examples are:
  - Discuss your favourite presenters and what made them good.
  - Brainstorm solutions to difficult questions that may come up.
  - Create a list of different ways you can present this data.
  - Come up with five pros and five cons for this proposal.

- Suggest a coffee break.

- Recap what has been covered so far.

- Signpost where you are: 'We have just covered ... we are now going to explore ...'

- Ask rhetorical questions. Why? Because they instantly raise the audience attention.

BODY LANGUAGE

Reading negative body language

Some body language can have a number of meanings so you will need to watch out for it in order to respond in the correct manner:

- Raising eyebrows
    - Disbelief
    - Invitation to respond
    - Interest
- Thumping the table
    - Emphasizing a point
    - Anger
- Clenched fist
    - Defensiveness
    - Aggressiveness

Positive body language

Positive body language from you accounts for 55 per cent of your message:

- An open, relaxed facial expression (beware the resting face which can look stern)

- Open hand gestures

- Arms slightly bent at the elbow, hands either holding something or loosely linked

- Gestures that emphasize your point.

Avoid

- Pointing – except to your presentation slides

- Jittery movements

- No movements at all
- Nodding your head when you are saying no and shaking your head when you are saying yes.

MANAGING YOUR AUDIENCE

When presenting, it is important that your audience knows what you expect from them and what they can expect from you. The following three charts enable you to do this:

GROUND RULES

- Phones off
- No hogging, frogging or bogging
- Confidentiality
- Keep to time
- Questions
- Park Issues

Ground Rules give the audience a framework of behaviour. They are a way of managing time and managing awkward situations. If you have this on a flipchart, it can be put up on the wall as a reminder and to refer to in times of need. Here is what you might say to accompany your points:

'We want to make sure that everyone is entirely focused on this presentation – there is a lot of information important to you *(building anticipation)*. Could you all take your phones out now and switch them off. You will have plenty of time during the breaks to deal with any messages you have. Thank you.'

'In order that we keep on track and get through the material so you leave here knowing everything you need to know about how to present confidently, can I ask that we give everyone a chance to speak; we keep our focus on the agenda and that we don't get too bogged down in detail?'

'We are going to be talking about sensitive issues in this presentation so it is important that we all agree to make what is said in this room entirely confidential. In this way, we can all be confident about being open and honest and, in so doing, we will get the best results from the session. Is that OK with everyone?'

'As we have such a tight schedule, when we have our breaks, please make sure you are back in your seats on time so that you don't miss anything.' *This lets them know you are not going to wait for latecomers.*

'I know this subject is very important to you all and will generate lots of questions. What I would ask is that you keep a note of any questions you have and we will deal with them in the Q&A section at the end. I'll write them on the Parked Issues Chart to make sure we remember everything.'

'Is everyone OK with these ground rules? Do we need to add any more? OK, let's begin.'

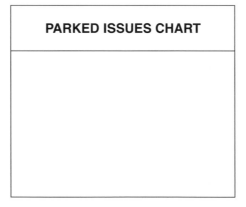

In a long presentation, it is easy for people to lose focus and a sense of where they are. In order to avoid the risk of them spending their mental energy wondering how much there is left to cover, simply put the agenda on a flipchart. By having your agenda displayed, it is easier for them to see how they are progressing and it can be used by you to sign-post shifts in subject matter: 'We have just covered preparation – the importance of laying the foundations for your presentation. Now we are going to move on to those moments of presentation desperation and how you can handle your nerves effectively.'

A Parked Issues Chart is an excellent way of capturing points that threaten to derail your presentation. It is important to acknowledge the point but not to indulge it. The Parked Issues Chart enables you to do just that. 'That's a great point David. However, it is outside the scope of today's presentation. Can we park this and deal with it at the end if we have time?' Then you simply make a note of it on the chart and refer to it later, should time allow.

You can be really creative with these with colours and images. You can also refer to them throughout the presentation. For example, if you find that someone is getting bogged down in too much detail, refer to the ground rules flipchart. To sign-post where you are in your presentation or to link you to the next stage, you can point to the agenda flipchart.

 COACH'S TIP

Keeping on track

Ground Rules, Agenda and Parked Issues Charts can help keep your presentation on track.

NOISY LUNCHES AND BREAKS

Sometimes your presentation will be at a time when refreshments are served. This can be very distracting as people become focused on what they are going to eat rather than on your message. Clattering cutlery only makes matters worse so, if possible, ensure there is a finger buffet and take a break for a few minutes while people plate up. They will not hear anything you say while they are focusing on whether to have the chicken or the quiche.

MAKING MISTAKES

You will be unique if you never make a mistake. You will be exceptional if you don't make a mistake when you present. The thing to remember is that making a mistake is OK – it's how you recover from it that is important. Here are some common mistakes with possible solutions:

Dropping your papers

- Use humour: 'That floored you!' or 'And for my next trick'.
- Calmly gather your papers, collate them and continue.

Your laptop crashing

- Use humour: 'Is there a doctor in the house?'
- Attend to the problem, and ask the audience's indulgence.
- Continue with your hard copy notes.

Losing your place

- Use humour: 'Can anybody guess what I was going to say next?'

- Take a deep breath and say 'Now, where was I?' and you should have bought yourself enough time to remember your place.

- Be honest and ask the audience where you were; they will usually help.

Saying the wrong thing

- Use humour: 'Sorry, Freudian slip.'

- Make a simple correction, i.e. 'profit, sorry, I mean revenue.'

Tripping up

- Use humour: 'Well, that was some trip!'

- Humour is the only way! Otherwise they will either feel sorry for you or think you are pompous. If you find it difficult to see the humour it may be a sign that you are taking yourself too seriously.

Stumbling over your words

- Either ignore it or carry on. It is only the thinking about it that causes you to stumble. If you simply engage with the content of your presentation and deliver from the heart, your words will flow. If it's good enough for Steve Jobs, it's good enough for you.

As you can see, humour can be very effective. However, timing is key. A badly timed joke can result in you being the joke, so practise some one-liners. Observe those people who do it well and see if you can deliver their punchlines in the way that they do – practise in private until you perfect your technique. If you are really interested in developing your ability to use humour, consider joining a stand-up comedy class.

> *We should not give up and we should not allow the problem to defeat us.*
>
> Abdul Kalam

NEXT STEPS

In this chapter you have learned how to use hecklers to enhance your credibility rather than seeing them as a threat. This includes how to deal with difficult people, handling awkward questions, as well as being mindful of body language so you address people's concerns openly rather than leave them feeling frustrated. You have learned how to deal with people who arrive late or who conduct their own conversations during your presentation. You have discovered techniques for dealing with an audience who don't have any questions and where you disagree with them. Finally, you have learned techniques to employ if and when you make a mistake during your presentation.

In the final section, you will explore some of the most powerful presentations to consolidate your learning and you will see a simple summary of the different phases of your presentation preparation.

👍 TAKEAWAYS

This is your opportunity to take stock of what you have learned from this chapter. You might want now to choose other chapters and exercises to focus on, or you can continue to work through the whole book if this fits your needs more.

Thinking about an upcoming presentation and your audience, what is your greatest fear about heckling?

Given what you have learned in this chapter, how do you propose you deal with these to the best effect?

What negative thoughts might you have about these hecklers and what would be a positive alternative you could employ?

CONSOLIDATING WHAT YOU HAVE LEARNED

In this book we have explored the various types of presentation and how to deliver them effectively. We have looked at the importance of knowing your audience, of having a positive mindset, of engaging and influencing your audience with integrity, as well as the nuts and bolts of your preparations and dealing with the unexpected.

Presentations can be enjoyable – for you and your audience. However, to get them right requires a significant amount of thought and planning. Mark Twain once said, 'If you want me to give you a two-hour presentation, I am ready today. If you want only a five-minute presentation, it will take me two weeks to prepare.' This quotation illustrates beautifully the importance of planning out what you say. Most of us only have a very short time to make our point so the words you choose and how you choose to say them can really impact your success.

The best presenters are those who are genuine and authentic – they believe in their message. People tend to have pretty good radars for nonsense so it is important to be honest and have complete belief in what you are talking about if you want to get their attention and win them over.

CONTINUOUS IMPROVEMENT

Having an attitude of continuous improvement – while appreciating how far you have already come – can really take your presentations to the next level. So, each time you do a presentation, do a self-evaluation. Consider what you did well – what enabled that? Was it better preparation? A more positive mindset? Were you more creative with your slides? Less creative with your slides?

Then think about what you would like to do differently if you had your chance all over again – what could be improved? Then, next time you are scheduled to stand in front of an audience, make sure that you focus on that improvement. In this way, you are continually progressing as a presenter.

Even the most polished of presenters aren't born that way – they learned from their mistakes and they became that way. So can you.

See Appendix 12 for checklist.

This book has already pointed you towards some presentations to take a look at. Here are some more which are recommended for your viewing:

'I Have a Dream' by Martin Luther King

One of the most iconic speeches ever made. He uses the emphatic repetition of the phrase 'I have a dream' throughout. Repetition of 'Let freedom ring', 'together' and 'free at last' are also used to powerful effect. Although this is very dated, its impact is still valid.

http://www.youtube.com/watch?v=I40NvGnpcKs

Jamie Oliver's Ted award-winning speech

Whereas Jamie breaks quite a lot of rules (his dress, speech, apologizing for himself), he more than makes up for this with his passion, structure and powerful content. He uses a strong opener before he introduces himself and then gives his credentials. He has a terrific use of the stage. Despite the huge audience, he manages to engage and interact with them. He also displays fabulous use of PowerPoint which is simple, powerful and completely supports his message to commanding effect. He also uses humour brilliantly. The Rule of Three is employed: 'friends, family, community' and he slaps his notes three times to emphasize his point. He looks at his screen but speaks to the audience. He uses silence for emphasis. He uses litotes – the ironical statement for dramatic effect. He also uses props and videos. Look at the way he walks around the upturned sugar – disdainfully – and this dramatically reinforces his point. It is really a masterclass in presentations – it is both uncompromising and compelling. He has thought of his entire audience: parents, accountants, politicians, the education system, the food industry. No wonder it won awards.

http://www.youtube.com/watch?v=jIwrV5e6fMY

Susan Cain: The power of introverts

In complete contrast to Jamie, Susan shows how you can give a powerful message without being in the least bit showy. As Jamie is gregarious, so Susan is contained. She talks about our culture of personality and how big personality seems to be so desirable for influencing in today's world but that this doesn't necessarily stack up. She demonstrates beautifully how it is possible to have impact as an introvert. She uses body language which displays both credibility and approachability and neatly punctuates her points with her hands – all in a very understated manner. She uses pauses, suspense and stories elegantly. She also employs the Rule of Three: 'my sense, my belief, my hope', 'privacy, freedom, autonomy' and finishes with three calls for action. She uses gentle humour and shows how speaking softly can still have impact.

http://www.ted.com/talks/susan_cain_the_power_of_introverts.html

Steve Jobs introducing iPhone 2007

One of Steve Jobs' stand-out speeches was in 2007 when he launched the iPhone. He started in silence, was very deliberate in his movements and these combined to build a level of expectation and excitement in the audience.

He used the Rule of Three technique to develop the expectation of three separate products – an iPod, a phone, and an internet communicator which, lo-and-behold, combine to form one device – the iPhone. He used power words terms such as 'revolutionary', 'phenomenal' and 'super-smart'. The PowerPoint slides are sublime in their simplicity.

http://www.youtube.com/watch?v=x7qPAY9JqE4

The speech that made Obama President

This clip comes with some useful analysis. Obama shows great use of body language (authority, approachability, strength and humility), the effective use of storytelling, repetition and structure. He shows a blend of contrast and finding common ground. The speech is described as electrifying.

http://www.youtube.com/watch?v=OFPwDe22CoY

COACHING SESSION 30

Presentation styles

Get yourself a coffee, sit down and study these presentations to see the patterns, techniques and approaches you admire. Think about which style works for you, what you can learn from each one that you can implement to create your own presentation style. What belief systems and attitudes do you think they hold that enable them to present in this way? Write down your top 10 learnings below:

One day at a time for the next ten days, implement one of the ideas in your day to day communication and interactions. Refine it so it becomes your own.

THE FIVE ELEMENTS OF PRESENTATION PREPARATIOIN

To summarise, preparing for an effective presentation has six main elements which can be summarised in the graphic below.

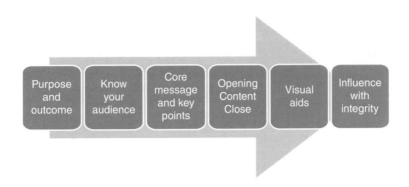

In his book *Presentation Zen*, Garr Reynolds talks about the importance of simplicity, clarity and brevity in making your presentation. Often less is more and too many people over-complicate their message both verbally and visually.

Throughout all of this is self-management. Making sure you have the magic mindset; that you know how to build rapport; and that you conduct your presentation with an attitude of wanting to help. In this way, you will connect more easily with your audience, influence more readily and enjoy more fully.

So, you have completed your coaching journey. But it doesn't end here. Do revisit this book often. Go through the highlights you made, the notes you took and remind yourself of the kind of presenter you would like to be. Enjoy becoming the best presenter you can be.

> *The meaning of the communication is the result you get.*
>
> NLP principle

APPENDICES

APPENDIX 1: RESOURCES

Images

Fotolia: http://en.fotolia.com/

Getty Images: http://www.gettyimages.co.uk/

IStock: http://www.istockphoto.com/

Books

Boothman, N. *Convince Them in 90 Seconds* (Workman Publishing, 2010)

Buzan, T. *Use your Head* (British Broadcasting Corporation, 1984)

Charvet, S. R. *Words that Change Minds* (Kendall/Hunt, 1997)

Cialdini, R. B., PhD. *Influence, The Psychology of Persuasion* (Harper Collins, 2007)

Duarte, N. *Slide:ology* (O'Reilly Media Inc, 2008)

Grinder, M. *Charisma, The Art of Relationships* (Michael Grinder & Associates, 2009)

Kevin, D. *The Diagrams Book – 50 Ways to Solve any Problem Visually* (LID Publishing, 2013)

Knight, S. *NLP at Work* (Nicholas Brealey Publishing, 2009)

McConnon, S. *Presenting with Power* (How to Books, 2006)

McDermott, I. & O'Connor, J. *Practical NLP for Managers* (Gower, 1996)

Reynolds, G. *Zen* (New Riders, 2012)

Sapolsky, R. M. *Why Zebras Don't get Ulcers* (Henry Holt and Company)

Shephard, K. Presenting at Conferences, Seminars and Meetings (Sage Publications, 2005)

Weekes, Dr C. *Self-Help for Your Nerves* (Thorsons, 1995)

White, R. *Networking Survival Guide* (Bookshaker, 2011)

Woolfrey, T. & Craven H. *An Inside Job* (Verity Publishing, 2012)

Woolfrey, T. 21 Ways and 21 Days to the Life You Want (Verity Publishing, 2008)

Woolfrey, T. *Think Positive, Feel Good* (Verity Publishing, 2008)

Yate, M. & Sander, P. *The Ultimate Business Presentations Book* (Kogan Page, 2003)

MP3s by Tricia Woolfrey

Download the following MP3s from the author's website: www.yourempoweredself.co.uk

- Sleep Well
- Relaxed and Confident (also available on CD)
- Stress Free

Emotional Freedom Technique (EFT) demonstration

www.self-help-resources.co.uk

Webinars

www.gotomeeting.co.uk

www.anymeeting.com

Creative language

http://www.rhymezone.com/ for rhyming words, thesaurus, synonyms, antonyms, matching consonant patterns and quotations.

http://www.brainyquote.com/ for quotations by author and topic

Survey software

http://www.surveymonkey.com

Speakers clubs

http://www.toastmasters.org/

http://www.the-asc.org.uk/

Online resources

The following resources can be downloaded from www.TYCoachbooks.com/Presenting:

- Presentation Preparation Checklist
- Personal Preparation Checklist
- Presentation Tooklit Checklist
- Presentation Time Plan
- Personal Evaluation
- Emotional Freedom Technique Instructions

Appendix 2: Presentation Preparation, Structure and Scheduling Checklists

General overview

Date and time	
Purpose of presentation	
Length of presentation	
Outcome (positively stated)	
Inform – Inspire – Teach – Explain – Reassure – Get Commitment – Gain Support – Win a Sale – Change Thinking – Elicit Input – Do – Change – Think – Feel – Understand – Commit	
Core message	
Key point 1	
Key point 2	
Key point 3	
Closing message	
Title	
Audience	
How many?	
How much do they already know?	
How might they feel about me?	
How might they be feeling before the presentation?	
How would I like them to feel during/following the presentation?	
Who are the key influencers?	
Who are the key supporters?	
Who are the key detractors?	
What are their hot buttons?	
What are their likely objections/difficult questions?	
What are they likely to approve of?	
What are their language patterns?	
What are their convincer strategies?	
Other	
Q&A during or after?	
Ratio of you versus I	
Number and length of breaks, if required	
Create presentation	
Spellcheck presentation and handouts	
Handouts	

Notes	
Time plan	
General flipcharts, if appropriate	
• Agenda	
• Ground Rules	
• Parked Issues Chart	
Room layout	
Bio and presentation to host	

Structure

Opening (10%)	
Engage (fact/develop anticipation/image/cartoon/quotation/question)	
Personal introduction	
Set framework and expectations (subject, agenda, ground rules, timings)	
Housekeeping (if appropriate: breaks, what to do in case of fire, toilets)	
Content (80%)	
Key point 1	
Key point 2	
Key point 3	
Methods of delivery	
• Talk	
• Group brainstorm	
• Pair work	
• Personal reflection	
• Demonstration	
• Flipchart	
• Slide	
• Text	
• Chart	
• Smart Art	
• Image	
• Case study	
• Template	
• Story	
• Metaphor	
• Power words	
• Other	

Summary 10%	
Summarize main points	
Strong close	
Q&A	
Call to action	
Next steps	
Contact details	

Scheduling

Put in diary	
Invite attendees, with venue, date, time and preparation they need to do	
Send reminder to attendees	
Book meeting room	
Book equipment	
• Projector	
• Screen	
• Laptop (if you don't have your own)	
• Whiteboard	
• Flipchart	
• Other	
Transport	
Lunch and refreshments	

An online version of this Presentation Preparation Checklist is available for your use from www.TYCoachbooks.com/Presenting

Appendix 3: Presentation Time Plan

Within the Time Plan remember to include:

■ breaks where appropriate

■ activities

■ visual aid cues

■ polls

■ flipchart content.

You can create a Presentation Time Plan and use it to identify any specific activities, points or visual aids you want to include.

Visual aid	Item/Note	Mins	Timing

An online version of this Presentation Time Plan is available for your use from www.TYCoachbooks.com/Presenting

Appendix 4: Presentation Toolkit

Laptop (with presentation on hard-drive)	
Laptop cable	
Memory stick	
Pointer	
Remote control for projector	
Extension lead	
PowerPoint slides	
Printout of PowerPoint slides	
A5 cards	
Handouts	
Water	
Tissues	
Leaflets/brochures	
Business cards	
Feedback forms if appropriate	
Delegate/attendee list	
Marker pens	
Pens	
Paper	
Highlighter pens	
Post-its ®	
Blu-Tack ®	

An online version of this Presentation Toolkit is available for your use from www.TYCoachbooks.com/Presenting

Appendix 5: Getting There Checklist

Estimated time	
Location address	
Venue contact information	
Parking at location	
Map to location	
Estimated travel time	
• Travel to venue (consider whether rush hour or not)	
• Train/traffic delays (be generous)	
• Buying petrol (with queue)	
• Queue for train ticket	
• Loading car for departure	
• Unloading car on arrival	
• Car park to reception to meeting room (allow for long walk and reception queues)	
• Setting up	
Total estimated time to presentation	

Appendix 6: Personal Preparation Checklist

Practise, practise, practise	
Energy	
• Well rested	
• Healthy, calming meal (avoid sugar, simple carbs and caffeine to minimize nerves)	
• Well hydrated	
Image	
• Audience and situation appropriate	
• No missing buttons, loose threads or droopy hems	
• Suits not shiny	
• Clothing clean and well pressed	
• No clashing colours or patterns	
• Shoes well-polished, price stickers removed	
• Hosiery free from ladders, holes or bobbly bits	
• Lint free	
• Hair and hands well-groomed	
• Flies and buttons done up (no chest hair or cleavage)	
• Discreet jewellery	
• Well applied make-up	
• Clothes do not show sweat	
• Outfit and grooming enhance confidence	
Confidence	
• Deep breaths	
• Visualize success	
• Empowering belief (power mantra)	
• EFT to manage any nerves (see www.self-help-resources.co.uk for a demonstration)	
• Eliminate negative voice	
• Positive anchor (smiling face or something else)	
• Imagine antagonists as vulnerable	
• Audience-focused rather than self-focused	
• Remind myself of your purpose and outcome	
• Have a strong start	

Body language	
• Relaxed and strong body language (stand tall, feet firmly on the ground, evenly spaced)	
• Relaxed facial expression	
• Walk purposefully	
• Hands calm and relaxed by your side	
• Hands and arms provide animation to support presentation	
Go to the toilet	
Enjoy	

An online version of this Personal Preparation Checklist is available for your use from www.TYCoachbooks.com/Presenting

Appendix 7: Webinar Presentation Checklist

Technical preparation – general	
Correct web browser	
Correct operating system	
Sufficient RAM	
What software do you need? And which version? i.e. Java, JavaScript, Adobe Flashplayer	
Hard-wired internet connection (need sufficient bandwidth for simultaneous screen sharing, video and audio conferencing – 700 kbps recommended)	
Other technical specifications specified by the provider?	
Webcam fully functioning	
Microphone fully functioning	
Use headset with microphone to reduce echo	
Resolution on your computer sufficient (generally 1280 ×1024 I)	
No firewall issues preventing connection with servers	
Read through and have to hand supplier's frequently asked questions	
Contact details for support in case of emergency (and local opening times)	
Presentation preparation	
As all presentation preparation with the following exceptions: • Practise your whole presentation with a friendly audience – you want to make sure all features are working effectively before you go live. Do this far in advance of the event so that you have plenty of time to remedy the situation. • When practising, make sure you can deliver the presentation without 'reading aloud' as this can sound very stilted and bore your audience, thereby increasing your drop-out rate.	
Technical preparation – specific	
Create conference	
Set up invitation using webinar service providr including confirmation emails and reminders	
Set up polls if appropriate	
Send out reminder 1	
Send out reminder 2	
Presentation preparation – before the event	
Turn off the sound on landline	
Turn off mobile	
Visit the toilet!	
Water and tissues available	
Get ready about 10 minutes before the start to ground yourself	
Open the files you will be presenting in advance of your meeting	

Five minutes before, dial into the conference and display a slide with a message saying 'The webinar will begin shortly'	
During the presentation	
Chat to the audience before the presentation starts to build rapport	
Have the mute button on during times you do not want questions from the audience	
When you do your introduction, make sure you set expectations appropriately: • What the presentation will cover • How they can interact (questions, comments, how they are feeling – see below) • How long the presentation will take	
If using video, keep centred, look at the camera rather than the screen and make sure you maintain positive body language.	

If your system has a 'mood' indicator, keep an eye on the mood of your audience. It will look something like this: ☺ ☹ If they seem unhappy it may be that you are talking too quickly, too slowly or that the message is confusing. Ask questions to clarify:
• 'Is this the right pace for you?' If no:
   • 'Do I need to speed it up?'
   • 'Do I need to slow it down?' (Remember that everyone will want a different pace – you will have to go with either the majority or your gut instinct as not everyone will vote.)
   • 'Can you hear me OK?'
   • 'Can everyone see the slides?'
• 'Are you with me so far?' If no, this is perhaps a good time to do a question and answer session. You can do this by unmuting or through the written question facility if you need to, i.e. 'I can see that some of you are a little confused – put in the question box the area you would like me to clarify.'	

If there is a technical problem with sound or screen, it may be your end or their end. Always practise in advance so the problem is not yours. If it is only one person, it is likely to be a problem their end and they may need to shut down their other applications. If not, it is a case of going through your troubleshooting guide to see what else it might be.	
Do keep the audience updated about where they are in the process. 'We have just covered X. We are now moving on to Y.' It helps people to keep focused and feel oriented to your presentation.	
Refer to slides regularly	
Project your personality	
Keep your eye on questions, mood and whether people are leaving. (It is natural to get one or two drop-outs but any more than that might be an indication that you are off track and are losing them.)	
Adjust your message accordingly.	
Remember to close by telling them what you have covered during the webinar and what you want them to do next.	

Appendix 8: Video Presentation Checklist

Purpose of video	
Who is it aimed at?	
What do they need/want?	
Brand values	
How do you want the audience to feel?	
Image is centred and framed appropriately	
Body language and voice project the message	
Clutter-free background	
Sound quality	
No outside noises	
Good lighting	
Steady image	
Sufficient lag at beginning and end	
Introduction and end slides	
Background music for introduction and end slides	
Appear relaxed and engaging	
Not obvious that reading from notes	

Appendix 9: Skype Presentation Checklist

Skype loaded	
Web camera	
Microphone	
Background is free from clutter	
Image centred on screen	
Eyes on the lens for the viewer to perceive eye contact	
Audio working well (headset and headphones recommended to avoid echo)	
Clear image, well lit	
Distracting noises eliminated	

Appendix 10: Radio Presentation Checklist

Listen to the show as part of your research – check for style of presentation, type of questions and level of audience interaction	
Clarify and rehearse main points	
Practise politician's tactic 'I think the important thing is …'	
Notes on single sheet (if allowed) or iPad (to avoid paper shuffling sounds)	
Remove jangly jewellery	
Voice well-modulated and supports the message	
Mouth correct distance from the microphone	
Keep head still	
Use interviewer's name	
Mention contact details, i.e. website address	

Appendix 11: Wedding Speeches Checklist

Father of the Bride	Groom	Best Man
• Thank guests	• Thank father of bride	• Read messages
• Thank helpers	• Thank guests	• Stories about groom
• Stories about bride	• Thank bride's parents	• Stories about couple
• Compliment bride	• Thank own parents	• Toast the couple
• Welcome groom to family	• Thank best man	
• Toast bride and groom	• Thank helpers	
	• Present mothers with bouquets	
	• Compliment bride	
	• Toast bridesmaids	
A5 cards – one point per card and one sentence per line. Number the cards		
Clear message		
Flow		
Variety in tone and pace		
Use pauses well		
Precision in speech		
Entertaining		
Respectful of people's feelings		
Non-offensive		
Not too long, not too short		

Appendix 12: Personal Post-presentation Evaluation for Continuous Improvement

	Terrible	Needs improvement	Not bad	Quite good	Excellent
Suitably dressed and well groomed					
Confident					
Appear relaxed and natural					
Good rapport with the audience					
Excellent eye contact					
Positive body language					
Appropriately facially expressive					
Lack of distracting habits					
Voice: Pace, Pitch, Projection, Pauses and Precision					
Articulate					
Make points clearly					
Free from uhs, ers, ahs, you-knows, and likes					
Handle questions well					
Well prepared					
Well organized					
Good structure					
Message is interesting and compelling					
Good and appropriate use of humour					
Keep to time					
Involve audience appropriately					
Deal with difficult people appropriately					
Good use of visual aids					

What specifically did you do well?

What will you do differently next time?

An online version of this Personal Post-presentation Evaluation is available for your use from www.TYCoachbooks.com/Presenting

ACTION PLAN

What are the five main points you have learned from this book which are going to have the biggest impact on your ability to present in the most impactful way? It is useful to make these SMART goals:

Specific

Measurable

Achieveable

Relevant

Time-bound

For example: 'I will list the various audience members, their specific hot-buttons, language patterns and convincer strategies and structure my presentation to accommodate these. I will have this done at least a week before the presentation so that I have plenty of time to practice.'

1.

2.

3.

4.

5.

Again, reflecting on each of the chapters of the book, think about what you will stop doing, start doing and continue doing over the coming days, weeks, months and year:

	Start doing	Stop doing	Ccontinue doing
Tomorrow			
This week			
This month			
This year			

QUICK HELP SHEET

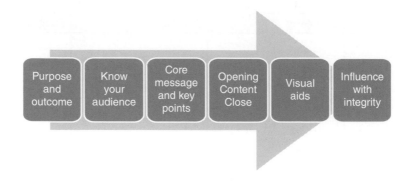

The four worst types of presenter			
The Waffler	The Preener	The Slideshow Bore	The Deer in the Headlights

Types of presentations

- **Business**: all employees, inter-departmental, departmental, clients, prospects, speaker introduction, webinars, videos, skype, radio, investor presentations
- **Social**: wedding, eulogy, thank you

Elevator pitch	
Basic Structure	Content options
• Name and business	• News
• What you do	• Interesting statistic
• Who you do it for	• Case-study
• Call to action	• Something topical
• Name and business	• Current project
• Memorable strapline	• A prop

Know your audience

- What problem do they face?
- How will they be feeling before your presentation (generally and specifically)?
- How much do they know?
- Who are key influencers and detractors?
- How are they likely to respond to your message?

Structure and content

- Set a clear outcome, positively stated (including inform, inspire, teach, explain, reassure, commitment, support, sell, change thinking, elicit input)
- Strong title
- 10% opening, 80% content, 10% closing
- Engage (e.g. a fact, develop anticipation, image or cartoon, a quote, a question)
- Personal introduction
- Set framework and expectations
- Content: decide on key points
- Anticipate questions
- Consider stories, metaphors. Illustrations, charts
- Summarise and strong close

Magic mindset

• Visualize success	• Reframe hostility
• Empowering beliefs	• Take the focus off you
• One conversation at once	• Clear outcome and purpose
• Confident body language	• A strong strart
• Deep breathing	• EFT to manage nerves
• Find a smiling face -- a positive anchor	

Engage and Influence

- Build rapport
- Be authentic
- Use appropriate language patterns, convincer strategies, pacing and leading
- Eye contact with whole audience
- Credible versus sympathetic and credible versus approachable
- Creative language
- Business case principles (why this, why now, who are stakeholders and what is the impact, outline proposed implementation, clear cost-benefit analysis)
- Benefits versus features
- Voice: the 5Ps: Pace, Pitch, Projection, Pause, Precision
- Appearance

Preparation

- Create time plan
- Choice of visual aid to support your message
- Equipment booked and tested
- Room layout decided
- Audience participation decisions and when to distribute handouts
- Spell check, know your numbers, practice content
- Spare markers and extra packs, hard copy and memory stick, power cable
- Practise timing

Hiccups and hecklers

- Reread Chapter 12
- Create and observe ground rules
- Observe and respond to body language
- Use humour
- Practise how you will deal with awkward questions or no questions
- Manage hogging, frogging and bogging

General

- Enjoy
- Use checklists
- Do personal post-presentation evaluation for continuous improvement

INDEX